JAPANESE TEA

A COMPREHENSIVE GUIDE

SIMONA SUZUKI

Published by Simona Suzuki through Kindle Direct Publishing Service in collaboration with Kyoto Obubu Tea Farms

ISBN: 9798414353195

Table of Content

Preface

This book is the result of many years living with and learning about Japanese tea. The journey started in a small Japanese tea town – Wazuka, Kyoto, where from the first moment, the magical scenery takes your breath away, and the taste of fresh green tea sweeps you of your feet.

More than 5 years have passed since then, every day pulling deeper and deeper into the world of tea. It started with learning about tea faming and processing by helping on the field and in the factory. Soon after that Japanese tea ceremony has invited to delve into the tea culture and build more understanding about the tea traditions. Then, about three years later, the door opened for a woman and a foreigner to join the Wazuka Tea Hand-Rolling Preservation Association. Making tea by hand, massaging and shaping fresh tea leaves is an inexplicable experience, that makes you appreciate the finished tea so much more. Lastly joining the Wazuka Tea Young Person's Association, that focuses on training the palette for tea flavors and aromas, enabled me to recognize and appreciate the regional differences of Japanese tea. All of that went along professionally working with Japanese tea and promoting it abroad. Meeting people from all around the world, who attended my hosted tea tours and events in Japan and abroad, made me realize how much interest there was in Japanese tea and how little information about it was available in English.

This book, therefore, is an attempt to provide a comprehensive source of Japanese tea, that explores it from different perspectives: from farming and processing, to different tea types and tea brewing, to history and culture. The book is based on my personal experience with Japanese tea as well as on the research by professionals in tea and related fields. I hope you will enjoy the book and will find it a useful source.

Acknowledgements

This book could not have come into existence without the support of many people, who care deeply about Japanese tea.

My greatest thank you goes to Kyoto Obubu Tea Farms, who inspired me and taught me so much about Japanese tea.

I am also really thankful to my life partner Sushi Suzuki, for all the support, advice and suggestions, that helped to shape this book.

A big thank you goes to several Obubu internship graduates. For help with research on Japanese tea to Kevin Alyono, Espen Fikseaunet, Maria-Alexandra Lulache, Jordan Ward, Jenny Swann and Mark Rohel. For help with the images to Anna Poian, Kevin Alyono, Kayleigh Innes and Veronica Hegar. For proofreading and shaping up the text to Kate Popham and Anna Poian.

I also feel a deep gratitude to my tea ceremony teacher Ikeda Sensei, who has shown me the approachable and bright side of Japanese tea ceremony, as well as a tea factory owner Okada-san, who has spent many hours with me conversing about tea.

Finally, I would like to thank all Wazuka town, for welcoming me and accepting me here. Only because of the warm and generous people in town I could have so many unique tea experiences, that gave base for this book.

1 Introduction

Tea has been an integral part of Japanese culture for hundreds of years. Introduced to Japan by Buddhist monks, tea has gradually developed its rituals and ceremonies, that have paved the way for it to the present day. In recent years, however, Japanese tea has been struggling to keep its ground domestically. Internationally, on the other hand, it has been gaining more and more interest due to the strong focus on healthy foods and lifestyles.

Information about Japanese tea in English, however, has remained fairly limited and quite sporadic. There are a few books dedicated to Japanese tea ceremony, and some world tea guides that briefly introduce Japanese tea and list several of its kinds. Until now there was no cohesive source in English that would focus specifically on Japanese tea and cover it from different angles. Japanese Tea: The Comprehensive Guide aims to fill the void and provide a comprehensive source on Japanese tea, by covering it from the leaf on the plant to the drink in the cup; and from the old days to the present times.

In this guide you will find the information about how Japanese tea is grown and processed. Following that, the guide will introduce common and unique kinds of Japanese teas. That will be followed by the chemical composition of the tea leaf and different brewing methods to draw out the flavor and nutrition components. Then the guide will turn to explore the history and culture of Japanese tea. Finally, it will introduce the common Japanese teaware used in tea brewing.

I hope you will find this guide useful as you embark on the Japanese tea journey.

2 Japanese Tea Farming

A tea plant can grow in the wild and survive for hundreds of years. To produce tea for human consumption, though, some level of farming is necessary, be it simply picking of the tea leaves or more advanced farming techniques, such as fertilizing, weeding, shading, etc. Traditionally tea used to be made by hand, but nowadays more and more tea production in Japan is mechanized and new techniques are invented to make tea farming more efficient. In this chapter we will look into the tea varieties and cultivars that are the most common in Japan as well as the life cycle that a tea plant goes through. Then we will move on to the annual tea farming cycle and will compare traditional and modern tea farming. Finally, we will delve into the debate on organic versus conventional farming.

2.1   Tea Varieties and Cultivars

Tea flower

The tea plant is a subtropical evergreen plant. Scientifically called Camellia Sinensis, it belongs to the camellia genus and is a sister of the beautiful blooming camellias. Camellia Sinensis is then subdivided into varieties and the two main varieties used for tea production are Camellia Sinensis Sinensis and Camelia Sinensis Assamica. The two varieties have some physical differences. Assamica plants can grow taller and will have bigger leaves, sometimes the size of a human palm, whereas Sinensis leaves tend to be much smaller[1]. They also vary by geographic distribution. Assamica variety mostly grows in India and Sri Lanka, whereas Sinensis variety is commonly found in China, Taiwan, Japan, etc.

The division between Sinensis variety and Assamica variety does not end here, as each variety can then be subdivided into cultivars. Cultivars are created by selecting and crossing tea plant cuttings to develop and strengthen their favorable qualities. In Japan alone there are several hundred different cultivars.

Zairai is the original botanical subdivision of Sinensis variety in Japan before any improvements from selective breeding. It is grown from seeds, which results in each plant being different from another. Zairai plants usually have different shooting speeds, which can be difficult for the farmers to manage, whereas cultivars made from cuttings are composed of clone plans with the same genetic information, so all plans of the same cultivar grow in the same way.

While the differences between cultivars may be less pronounced than between varieties, they may still vary in leaf color, shape, even shooting time and of course taste profile. According to the Japanese Ministry of Agriculture, Yabukita cultivar is the most common in Japan and accounts for around 74% of all Japanese tea fields[2]. It was bred in Shizuoka at the beginning of the 20th century and was favored for its high yield, umami taste and resistance to frost. A few other lesser-known cultivars that are responsible for 2%-6% of Japanese tea include Yutaka Midori, Saemidori, Samidori, etc.

Yabukita cultivar

Saemidori cultivar

2.2   Tea Plant Life Cycle

In the wild tea plants can grow for several hundred or even several thousand years. However, for commercial production, tea plants between 5-40 years provide the highest yield. So in Japan tea plants tend to be planted and replanted every 40-50 years.

Tea plants can be propagated in one of the two ways: from seeds or from cuttings. At the beginning of tea cultivation tea used to be propagated only from seeds. The seed from one tea plant would carry only half of that plant's genetic information. The other half came from the tea plant that had provided the pollen to the tea flower of the first tea plant. The result of this genetic recombination is that plants propagated from seeds will differ from one another both in the physical appearance and in taste, that they carry in their leaves. A tea field with plants propagated from seeds will be less predictable and therefore more difficult to manage.

Tea seed and tea seed pouches

Propagation can also be done though cuttings, where a cutting of a branch (usually about 5cm long with one leaf) is taken from the mother plant. A cutting carries forward all its mother plants genetic information, so effectively it is a clone of the mother plant. A tea field with tea plants propagated from cuttings rather than seeds will have more uniform plant behavior and taste. So nowadays propagation via cuttings is the method favored by most tea farmers in Japan.

Tea planting, by Kyoto Obubu Tea Farms

In Japan at the end of the spring harvest, when the young shoots have matured, tea plant branches are cut for propagation and divided into 5cm segments with one leaf on each. The cutting is then planted in the nursery to develop a root system, where it will be looked after for 1-2 years. When the cutting has developed more roots, it is transplanted into its permanent location. One tea field row is usually created from two rows of cuttings that are planted in a zigzag fashion. Each year young tea plants are trimmed to create a wider branch structure. Depending on the tea field condition young tea plants could be harvested from the 3rd year in their permanent field, but for commercial production they start to give a good harvest from around their 5th year. While for tea production only the new growth is harvested, about every 3 years a deep cut into its mother leaves and branches is performed to rejuvenate the plant and encourage new branch growth. At about 40 years the tea plant production level diminishes. It is then a common practice to pull out the older plants and replace them with new ones.

2.3 Annual Tea Farming Cycle

Everyone is probably aware that to make tea, tea leaves need to be harvested from a tea plant. Harvesting, however, is not the only farming activity. In addition to harvesting tea, farmers also undertake trimming, fertilizing, weeding, pest and disease control, shading, and other activities. Tea farmers look after their tea fields throughout the year, and in Japan most of the tea farming activities usually occur between March and November.

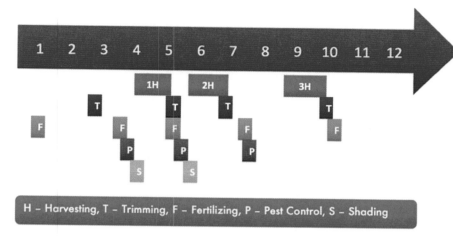

| 1 | 2 | 3 | 4 | 5 | 6 | 7 | 8 | 9 | 10 | 11 | 12 |

1H   2H   3H

T   T   T   T

F   F   F   F   F

P   P   P

S   S

H – Harvesting, T – Trimming, F – Fertilizing, P – Pest Control, S – Shading

Annual Japanese tea farming activities in Kyoto region

One bud and two leaves

Harvesting is one of the main tea farming activities. Harvesting refers to tea leaf collection for tea production (if tea leaves are picked but not used for tea production, that would be called trimming or pruning). For high grade tea in Japan usually one bud and two leaves of the new shoot are harvested. The remaining tea leaves of the new shoot below that (usually 3rd, 4th and 5th leaf) are harvested later and made into lower grade tea.

In most regions of Japan tea can be harvested up to 3 times a year. While some artisan tea farms, that produce only the highest-grade tea such as Gyokuro or ceremonial grade Matcha, may harvest tea only in spring, most tea farms complete at least 2 or 3 harvests per year.

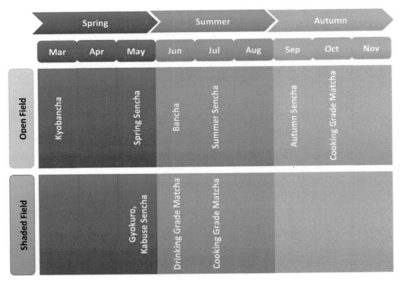

Japanese tea harvesting seasons in Kyoto region

Spring is the main harvesting season and everyone awaits it with anticipation. Dormancy period created by cold weather allows the tea shoots to gather more nutrients leading to more developed and rich taste. Due to this, spring season tea is usually more valued and sold at a higher price. Tea harvested in the summer and autumn seasons tends to be cheaper.

Depending on the region spring harvest usually starts between the middle of April and the middle of May. Some southern prefectures such as Okinawa may be able to start spring tea harvest as early as March. Spring harvest of higher grade tea (Sencha and Matcha) usually continues until the end of May or the beginning of June. That is usually followed by the harvest of the leaves for lower grade tea, called Bancha.

The second harvest of higher grade tea starts around the end of June and continues to the second half of July. Finally, the third harvest usually starts in the second half of September and can continue all the way until the beginning of November.

Tea leaves continue to grow through the warm part of the year and need to be picked at regular intervals. Higher grade tea of later seasons, such as summer and autumn, as well as lower grade tea tend to receive lower price, so instead of making picked tea leaves into tea some farmers return it to the ground and use it as fertilizer. Such activity, when tea leaves are picked but not processed into tea, is called trimming or pruning.

Deep trimming

Tea trimming is usually carried after the main harvesting seasons to cut down the remaining parts of the new shoots that had matured and to encourage new growth. It addition to that, it helps to keep the tea plants at a manageable height. Trimming also helps to keep the tea plants in shape. Therefore, tea plants can be trimmed not only from the top but also from the sides, to ensure an easy passage during harvesting and other farming activities. In addition to the routine trimming between the harvesting seasons, about once every 3 years at the end of the spring harvest a deep trimming into the tea plant mother leaves and branches is performed to encourage new branch growth. Summer and autumn harvests in that year would be skipped to allow rejuvenation of the tea plant.

In general tea plants prefer well drained and acidic soil between 5.5pH – 4.5pH[3]. In the wild, the tea plant gets its nutrients from the soil directly around it. However, to provide a good yield for commercial tea production, tea plants need more nutrition – so are usually supplemented with fertilizers. Fertilizers help to encourage plant growth and create more developed flavors in the leaf. The main components of the fertilizer for tea plants include nitrogen, phosphorus and potassium. Some research suggests, that increase in the amount of nitrogen fertilizer is followed by an increase of L-theanine in the tea leaves[4], which gives tea umami taste.

There are two types of fertilizers: natural and synthetic. Natural fertilizers are usually made from plant and animal remains (such as canola seed remains or ground animal bones), as well as manure. Synthetic fertilizers are thus chemically designed. Natural fertilizers first need to be broken into simple compounds, and that takes time. Synthetic fertilizers, on the other hand, are quicker for the plant to absorb. The choice of the fertilizer depends on each tea farmer and their tea farm management techniques. Fertilizers are usually applied a few weeks before the harvest as well as routinely in other seasons of the year, to ensure continued nutrition for the tea plant. Nowadays in Japan, machinery will often be used to mix the fertilizer deeper in the ground, where the roots of the tea plant can easily reach it.

A tea farm is a nurtured part of nature and because of that it provides an inviting environment for insects and weeds. Some insects cause no harm for tea and can peacefully coexist. Others, though, may feed on the delicious tea leaves. Some of the common insects causing damage to the tea leaves are: tea leaf hopper, tea leaf roller, red spider mite, etc. Nowadays pesticides will be used to prevent the dangerous insects or to eliminate them if already present. Use of pesticides is highly regulated and each country has their own standards. Tea farmers in Japan will usually follow the regulations.

Herbicides can also be used to control the number of weeds in the field. If herbicides are not used, manual weeding will take place to ensure that the weeds don't overwhelm the tea plant or get mixed in with the harvested tea leaves.

Weeds in the tea field

Another threat for the tea plant is frost. Frost usually forms because of the temperature difference between daytime and night-time, which causes condensation on the tea leaves that freezes in negative temperatures. The biggest danger comes in spring when the new tea shoots start to come out. New shoots are soft and delicate, so they can easily be damaged by the frost, which would impact the amount and quality of the harvest. The most common way to fight the frost is a mechanical fan that is elevated about 6-8m[5] above the tea field and helps to bring the warm air from the high level to the tea leaf level, keeping the temperature around the tea leaves more consistent. An alternative to mechanical fans is a sprinkler system, common in Kyushu, that continuously sprays water on the leaves, keeping the temperature above 0°C.

Mechanical fans in the tea field

Once the healthy new tea shoots start to come up, some of the tea farmers in Japan shade them from the sun. Shading helps to create more umami taste, as it helps to keep more L-thianine in the leaf. L-thianine is one of the amino acids, that mostly develops at the roots of the tea plant[6]. In the tea leaves it can be reduced back to the previous components, which, when exposed to sunlight, help to form catechins[7]. Catechin is a compound that gives tea an astringent or bitter taste. Shading, therefore, helps to maintain umami taste and prevent the creation of astringent taste in a tea leaf. Depending on the kind of tea, the plant can be shaded for between 2 – 4 weeks. For Kabuse Sencha it usually takes 2 weeks, for Gyokuro – 3 weeks and for Matcha – 4 weeks. The shading can be applied directly on a tea plant or it can be elevated above a tea plant in a shelf style – a more traditional shading method.

A tea field with direct shading, by V.Hegar

2.4 Traditional versus Modern Tea Farming

In Japan tea has been grown and cultivated for several hundred years. Through time farming techniques have changed and evolved and of these, harvesting methods have probably changed the most. Until the beginning of the 20th century, tea in Japan was picked the traditional way – by hand. Wives and daughters of the tea farming families would get up at sunrise and rush to the fields to start the tea picking, which they would do until sunset. This traditional tea harvesting was labor intensive and had little productivity.

The next stage in history was to cut the new shoots with shears with a bag attached, into which the leaves would fall directly. This helped to increase productivity by about 10 times.

Following that, a few decades ago portable machines for tea harvesting were introduced. A portable harvesting machine would be held by two people hugging a row of tea plants from each side. This is still a popular harvesting method today, especially in the mountainous areas of Japan. In flatlands, though, man-driven machines have become more popular. These machines stand over the row of tea plants and cut their tips directly into a container inside a machine. Some areas are introducing even more automated machines, that hover over the rows and pick the tea by sliding on the rails built inside the tea field. In this case all that a tea farmer needs to do is to press a button to start the machine and then it does the job itself. Thanks to all of these modern tea harvesting techniques, Japan is known for its beautifully manicured rows of tea, which are incredibly picturesque. Historically, when the tea was picked by hand or with the shears, tea plants grew more sporadically without forming these beautiful rows.

Another difference brought by time is the shading technique. In the old days, tea plants were shaded with natural dry reeds. Reeds, however, have to be replaced every year and their preparation is rather time consuming. So these days, natural reeds are often replaced by plastic covers that can be applied over and over again.

Finally, because of the developments in the chemical industry, we now have more advanced synthetic fertilizers and pest control substances. While some see it as a blessing allowing more productivity, others see it as a curse.

Tea picking by hand, by K.Innes

Portable harvesting machine, by Kyoto Obubu Tea Farms

16

Natural reed shading

Synthetic shading

2.5 Conventional versus Organic Tea Farming

As we have seen, the last century has brought a lot of changes in tea farming to help make it more productive and efficient. In recent years, reliance on synthetic substances in farming has been contested, and organic farming has been suggested as an alternative.

Today, organic farming is internationally regulated and there are strict standards for organic certification. Organic farming in a broad sense refers to a whole production system that aims to 'sustain the health of soils, ecosystems and people' [8]. In practice, organic farming involves crop cultivation without genetically modified seeds, synthetic fertilizers and pesticides[9]. Instead, it relies on naturally occurring substances for plant nutrition, on biodiversity for pest control and on manual labor for weed control. Organic farming is often favored due to a perceived positive effect of food safety and environmental sustainability.

Organic farming method, however, is not without its flaws. Organic agriculture seems to have lower input costs as it does not need to reply on costly synthetic substances. However, the yield of organic production tends to be lower than that of conventional production[10]. Hence, to produce the same amount of food organic farming method tends to require more resources: land and labor.

The food safety and nutritional superiority of organic products is also contested as evidence on nutritional difference remains limited[11]. Also, contrary to popular belief organic does not equal pure. Even if synthetic substances are not permitted in organic farming, residue is often found in organic produce (some synthetic substances travel easily through air and water and can be easily absorbed from the surrounding environment). Even in conventional farming, strict standards for residue levels are set and tea farmers in Japan tend to follow it to the letter.

A debate on the organic versus conventional farming is a difficult one with no easy answer. While overreliance on synthetically substances can be at odds with health and environment, organic farming is not without its flaws and does not automatically equal a superior product when compared to conventional produce.

Talking about Japanese tea specifically, according to the IFOAM, only about 0.4% of farming land in Japan is used for organic production[12]. Domestic demand of organic produce remains rather small, but because of growing international demand for organic tea, some tea farmers turn to the use of organic farming methods.

However, the switch from conventional farming to organic is not immediate. 3 years without the use of synthetic substances are required before a farm becomes eligible for organic certification[13].

Organic tea farmers in Japan rely on natural materials and biodiversity in tea farming. Popular choices for fertilizers include canola seed meal, animal and fish bone meal, and animal manure. Pest control on organic tea farm is based on biodiversity and farmers mostly rely on spiders, lady bugs and other predatory insects to suppress the pest population. Weed control is predominantly managed with manual labor.

3 Japanese Tea Processing

Essentially, all tea: black, green, oolong, etc. can be made from the same tea plant, it all depends on how the tea leaves are processed. The finished tea is assigned to one of those categories based on the level of oxidation in its leaves. In this line, green tea means non-oxidized tea, black tea is fully oxidized and oolong is semi-oxidized.

Green tea is the most common type of tea in Japan. To achieve the common flavor of Japanese green tea, harvested tea leaves need to be processed in a certain way before we can brew them. If out of curiosity you tried to brew freshly harvested tea leaves, you would find that the taste is completely different from what we expect from a regular tea. Tea processing is necessary to both help develop the tea flavors as well as to preserve it for later use. Japanese green tea processing is commonly divided into primary and secondary.

Japanese tea processing flow

This chapter will first look through the primary processing steps essential in Japanese green tea production. It will then go on to introduce the secondary processing steps that are mostly used for enhancing the physical appearance of the tea leaves and altering the taste. Finally, it will look into some additional steps that some popular Japanese green teas might go through as well as into how tea processing has changed throughout history.

3.1 Primary Processing Steps

Most Japanese green tea will go through primary processing, and there are 3 key steps. The first and the most important is steaming. It is used to stop the oxidation in the fresh tea leaves and to preserve their green qualities. When exposed to air, harvested tea leaves will start to oxidize, the most visible result of which is the change of color from green to brown. To prevent this from happening, tea leaves need to be heated to deactivate the enzymes that aid the oxidation. The steaming method is unique to Japan, other green tea producing countries rely mostly on pan-frying to stop oxidation.

Steaming is a very short process that only takes seconds (usually in the range of 15s-200s). Depending on the time used, tea steaming can be called light, medium and deep, however the lines are not clearly drawn and the naming is usually left for the farmer to decide.

In addition to stopping the oxidation, steaming will also soften the tea leaves and make them easier to handle. The deeper the steaming the easier the leaves break in the later processing steps, so deep steamed tea tends to result into more broken tea leaves that bring out darker color and stronger taste of tea. In contrast, light-steamed tea leaves will give lighter and clearer color as well as a crisper taste.

After steaming the tea leaves are rolled, this is the longest step in the primary processing and it can take several hours. It is necessary for shaping the tea leaves, releasing aroma, and reducing moisture content. There are three stages of rolling: rough, middle and fine. Rough rolling is performed to dry extra moisture gained from steaming. Middle rolling is for breaking the cell structure inside the tea leaf, so the flavors can be easily extracted to a cup when the tea is steeped. Fine rolling is for creating the shape of the tea leaf - the beautiful straight needle that Japanese tea is known for.

During the rolling process tea leaves are handled at a warm temperature, so the moisture in the tea leaves decreases little by little. To preserve the tea for a longer time, though, tea leaves need to be further dried until the moisture content is around 5%[1]. Nowadays a drying machine has a rotating conveyer belt that slowly moves the leaves inside it and dries them for another 20-30 minutes[2]. It is interesting to note that the tea weight at the end of primary processing makes only about 1/5 of the fresh tea leaves weight.

Steaming machine at the Center for Education and Research in Field Sciences, Shizuoka University

Rough rolling machine at the Center for Education and Research in Field Sciences, Shizuoka University

Middle rolling and twisting machine at the Center for Education and Research in Field Sciences, Shizuoka University

Middle rolling machine at the Center for Education and Research in Field Sciences, Shizuoka University

Fine rolling machine at the Center for Education and Research in Field Sciences, Shizuoka University

Drying machine at the Center for Education and Research in Field Sciences, Shizuoka University

Aracha

At the end of the primary process we get aracha, a.k.a. crude tea, which contains the whole bouquet of tea elements: leaf segments, fannings, stems. Aracha can already be brewed to make tea and because all parts of one leaf are used, it creates a beautiful natural taste. However, you will rarely find it on the market, because it is usually perceived to be an unfinished product with lesser visual appeal and taste. So it will often be sent for secondary processing to improve its visual quality and alter the taste.

3.2   Secondary Processing Steps

To meet the demand of Japanese tea market for the uniform appearance and consistent taste of tea, most Japanese green tea will go through secondary processing. Secondary processing usually involves such steps as sorting, cutting, blending, firing, etc., the result of which is shiagecha, a.k.a refined tea.

As mentioned before, at the end of the primary processing aracha will include all parts of the leaf: leaf segments, fannings, stems. A sorting step is used to create uniform appearance of tea by separating the bigger leaf particles, valued the most by the tea industry, from the stems, that disrupt the uniformity of dark green color with their light green shades, and fannings, that can impair the taste and make it more unbalanced, since they release flavors quicker than the bigger leaf segments.

Shiagecha

The most common sorting method involves a machine with a mesh inside. When the mesh is shaken fannings and stems fall through the vertical gaps and leaf segments remain on the mesh. If the leaf and the stem size and shape are quite similar and it is quite difficult to separate them with a shaking mesh, a color recognition machinery may be used, which can tell the difference between darker leaves and lighter stems. After tea leaves are separated from the stems and fannings, a cutting process may be added to further ensure the uniform size of the leaves.

Once we have the uniform appearance the next step is to create a consistent taste, which is achieved through blending. The Japanese tea industry values consistency and expects the tea to taste the same each year. However, tea is a product of nature and year-by-year its taste may differ a little depending on the weather conditions the tea leaves grow in. Blending tea from several sources helps to ensure that even if one source has been affected, the final tea product will not change significantly.

Blending may also be used to adjust the price of tea, where mixing tea from several seasons (such as adding summer tea leaves into spring tea) can make the tea more economical. Blending can also be used for marketing purpose, where adding tea leaves from one region into the mix of another (such as famous Uji tea into Shizuoka or Kagoshima mix), will increase its ranking and value.

Finally, aracha tends to have a rather green and vegetal aroma and taste. To adjust it, firing process, in Japanese called hiire, can be used. Tea leaf firing is a process similar to roasting, but shorter and with lower heat. It will add a light toasted aroma and taste making the tea more pleasant to some palettes.

As seen in this chapter secondary tea processing helps to create a more uniform and consistent tea for selling en masse. Aracha, on the other hand, that celebrates unique and natural qualities of tea, can provide a tea with a more distinct personality.

3.3   Additional Processing for Specific Teas

Most common Japanese green teas will go through the primary processing and often secondary processing. There are some teas that wander off the main path and have some additional processing steps until they become a finished product. Two main examples we can look into are: roasting for Hojicha and grinding for Matcha.

Roasting can be added after the primary or secondary processing. In fact, roasting can be applied to any part of a tea leaf: leaf segments, fannings or stems. During the roasting process tea is heated in a rotating drum at about 200°C[3], which results in the tea a gaining pleasant roasted aroma and brown color (it still belongs to the green category, though).

Hourokn – tea roasting pan

27

Matcha stone mill at Meiko Chagyo

Another additional process, grinding, is used for Matcha – powdered Japanese green tea. The primary process of Matcha is altered a bit in the sense that the rolling step is missing. Grinding takes place after the secondary processing, when the raw material for Matcha, called Tencha, is ground into powder. Traditionally Matcha used to be ground by granite stone mills of about 30cm in diameter. This way, however, can only produce about 40g of Matcha per hour. An industrial rolling ball method, with ceramic balls crashing into each other when shaken, on the other hand, can grind about 10kg of Matcha per hour. Nowadays the grinding process creates fine powder with the particle size of about 10 microns.

3.4   Traditional versus Modern Tea Processing

Tea processing by hand

Nowadays, most Japanese tea is processed in factories. Like in tea farming, though, traditionally Japanese tea used to be processed by hand. It was a long and strenuous process, that required around 6 hours of continuous handling of the tea leaves to complete the primary process. The tea leaves would go through the same processing steps as we know today, just that it all used to be done by hand. In fact, tea processing machinery was inspired by the hand movements and tried to resemble them as much as possible. When the tea processing machines were introduced at the beginning of the 20th century[4] they could only handle small amounts of tea – around 30kg - at a time. As tea industry grew, through time, tea processing machines got bigger and bigger, and today some machines can handle up to 250kg of fresh tea leaves at once.

4 Japanese Tea Types

You know that in Japan the most common tea is green. However, that does not mean just one kind of tea, as green tea can be divided into many different kinds of teas. Some of the most famous ones include Sencha, Gyokuro, Matcha. This chapter will look through some of the most common Japanese teas (that belong to the green tea category) as well as some more rare and unique teas within and outside the green tea category.

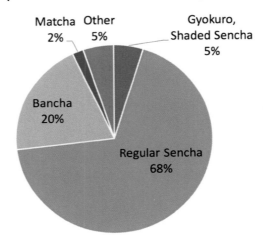

Japanese Tea Production by Kind

Japanese tea production by kind, data from Japanese Tea Instructors Association (2015)

4.1 Common Japanese Green Teas

Sencha

Sencha is one of the most popular Japanese teas. It accounts for about two thirds of all tea made in Japan. However, it has a comparatively short history of a few hundred years. In 1738 Nagatani Souen, one of the most prominent tea manufacturers in Uji, invented Sencha production method[1]. Sencha can be made from tea leaves grown in full sunshine or shaded (in which case it would take the name of **Kabuse Sencha** or Kabusecha). In general, the taste of Sencha tends to have some astringent and umami tones. Depending on how the tea plant was grown and when it was harvested one or the other can come out more strongly. Traditionally Sencha used to be brewed in a kyusu, although, nowadays ready-made bottled Sencha from a vending machine has become quite popular.

Gyokuro

Gyokuro is another famous Japanese tea, and its name can be read as 'jade dew'. The story has it that it was discovered by chance, when a tea merchant Yamamoto Kahei VI came to Uji to study Tencha production. He saw that the tea plants for Tencha were covered to protect them from frost, and was the first to apply this technique in Sencha farming[2]. The result was a richer and sweeter taste; and a new tea – Gyokuro – was born. Gyokuro is made in spring, and the tea plants are covered for about 3 weeks before harvesting. Some traditional tea farms still harvest Gyokuro by hand. When brewed it gives a pale liquor and a rich umami taste, that continues for several brews.

Bancha

Bancha is a lower grade tea that makes up nearly one third of Japanese tea. It is made from the bigger and more mature leaves of the new shoots and is usually harvested after the first harvest of Sencha or Tencha. Because it is made from the leaves that have been exposed to more sunshine, it tends to be more astringent than higher grade teas. It also gives base for other wonderful Japanese green teas, such as Genmaicha or Hojicha.

Genmaicha

In Japan teas are mostly enjoyed pure, not flavored. **Genmaicha** is one of the very few exceptions to this rule. It is usually created by mixing Bancha tea leaves with roasted rice, but sometimes Sencha leaves can be used too. Historically its purpose was to offer a more economical option for tea, as mixing tea leaves with rice lowered the cost and made the tea last longer. Nowadays it is a popular tea in Japan and around the world. Sometimes you can even find it with Matcha powder mixed inside to provide a stronger color and taste (called Matcha iri Genmaicha).

Hojicha

Hojicha is a roasted Japanese green tea. Usually Bancha will be used as its material, but sometimes you can find Hojicha made from Sencha or Kukicha. The tea leaves (or stems) will be roasted over a high heat to give new roasted flavors and aromas. Even if its leaf and liquor color is brown it is still considered green tea, as it is made from green tea to begin with.

Matcha

Matcha is one of the most famous Japanese teas, and is often ascribed super food qualities. It is a powdered tea full of nutrients. Tea leaves used for Matcha are grown in the shade for 4 weeks before harvesting. Then they are steamed and dried, separated from the stems, cut into smaller segments and ground to powder. Traditionally Matcha is prepared in a bowl where the green powder would be mixed with hot water and whisked to create a smooth foam on its surface. Nowadays Matcha has become a popular cooking ingredient and you can find it in many sweet and savory dishes.

4.2 Unique and Rare Japanese Teas

While the teas listed above are the most common in Japan, there are some beautiful rare and unique teas too. They may be made more regionally or by using different processing methods. Green tea is the most popular, but Japan does make other kinds of tea, such as oolong, black or dark.

Green Teas

Tencha

Tencha is mostly known as a material for Matcha, but it can also be brewed on its own. However, it is quite difficult to find Tencha on the market, as most of it will be used to produce Matcha. Tea leaves for Tencha are only steamed and dried. As it skips the rolling step, that would break the cell walls inside the leaf, Tencha gives a rather light infusion. To reach intensity in taste, comparable to other Japanese loose-leaf teas, the amount of tea leaves and steeping time would need to be adjusted.

Kukicha

Kukicha is a common but a bit unusual Japanese tea, as it is made from the stems rather than the leaves. Kukicha started as a by-product of Matcha and Sencha production, when for higher grade teas stems were separated from the leaves. Kukicha, however, has become a wonderful tea in its own right, with a lighter taste which makes a good introduction to the world of Japanese teas. You can find Kukicha in both a green and roasted form.

Konacha

Konacha is a lower grade powder tea. It usually refers to the tea fannings and dust – a by-product of tea sorting process. It tends to be sold at a lower price and is often intended for teabag production and other mass use.

Kyobancha

Kyobancha is a roasted tea, that sometimes can also be called Iribancha. It is mostly made in Kyoto region and thus 'Kyo' in its name comes from Kyoto. It is different from other roasted teas, as it is made from mature leaves that are usually harvested in March. Then, similar to Tencha, the leaves are only steamed and dried, and finally roasted. Kyobancha is nearly caffeine free, as the mature tea leaves have a little amount of caffeine. Producing Kyobancha from mature leaves also makes it a cheap and more economical tea.

Kamairicha

Kamairicha, is a Japanese green tea made by using the pan-frying method instead of steaming. This method originated in China and today is still used in some areas of Kyushu island. To make Kamairicha, tea leaves will be pan-fried and rolled repeatedly until fully dry. The result is usually curled tea leaves, commonly known as **Tamaryokucha**. (Just to add a note that Kamairicha can result in both Tamaryokucha or Kamanobicha – tea with straight needle shaped leaves. In addition to that, Tamaryokucha can be made by using both pan-frying or steaming methods).

Sanpincha – is a Japanese jasmine tea. While most Jasmine tea is famously made in China, Japan does make some too, mostly in its southern islands of Okinawa. The origins of Sanpincha go a few hundred years back to when the processing method was brought from China. Today Sanpincha is made by adding jasmine petals to Sencha tea during dying process.

Black Teas

Wakoucha

Moving outside of the green tea category, **Wakoucha** is a Japanese black tea. We know that green tea is the most popular in Japan, but some tea farmers do make black tea as well. Black tea is made through a completely different process. Tea leaves are usually withered, then they are rolled and bruised to oxidize; and finally dried to finish. While usually Camelia Sinensis Assamica variety would be used in black tea production, in Japan Camelia Sinensis Sinensis is commonly the base of it, which results in a delicate taste.

Oolong Teas

Oolong is a semi-oxidized tea. It is not very common in Japan, but there are some tea farmers that appreciate it and make it. At first, tea leaves are left to wither. Then they are rolled (more lightly than black tea), and sent to drying, that also stops the oxidation. While oolong includes a wide range of teas from light to dark, Japanese oolongs tend to be darker in nature.

Oolong

Dark Teas

Japan also makes some post-fermented dark tea. Shikoku island is the most abundant and makes a few different kinds. One of them is **Awabancha**, or pickled tea, from Tokushima prefecture. Tea leaves picked in July are boiled, rolled, and sealed in a barrel for fermentation, which can take a few weeks. When brewed the tea gives a rather sour infusion.

Goishicha is another fermented tea from Kochi prefecture. Tea leaves picked in July are steamed and pressed during fermentation process. At the end of fermentation pressed leaves are cut into small black bricks and dried. Like Awabancha it also tends to have a sour taste.

Ishidzuchi Kurocha is yet another fermented tea from Ehime prefecture. It is steamed and allowed to ferment first. Then it is rolled, fermented again and finally dried. It tends to have a sour taste too.

Batabatacha is one more fermented tea, that is produced in Toyama prefecture. The leaves are steamed, rolled, then placed in boxes for fermentation and finally dried. The brew of this tea is traditionally whisked until it gets frothy when drunk at wedding or funeral ceremonies. Unlike other fermented teas it tends to have an earthy rather than sour taste.

4.3 Japanese Tea by Harvesting Season

Japanese tea can also be classified by harvesting seasons. Below are the descriptions of how tea in different seasons is called.

Ichibancha, Nibancha, Sanbancha

Ichibancha means the first harvest and refers to tea made in spring season. These teas tend to be more valued, because the tea plant had more time to store the nutrients before shooting the new buds, so the tea tends to have a richer and more developed flavor. Freshly made spring tea can alternatively be called **Shincha**, which literally means "new tea".

Nibancha means second harvest, and it is used to describe tea made in summer season. Summer tea is usually regarded as lower grade and tends to sell at a lower price.

Sanbancha – third harvest tea is often called **akiban** or **akiten** that refers to tea made in the autumn season. The later the season the lower the price gets, so farmers have little incentive to make it. Nonetheless, autumn tea leaves are often chosen for pet-bottle tea and cooking grade Matcha production.

Haruban. Tea farming usually stops in late autumn, but the tea plant continues to grow and there are still leaves that need to be trimmed before the spring season. Those coarse low-grade leaves that survived through the winter are harvested around March. Haruban, therefore refers to spring Bancha, where haru in Japanese means spring and 'ban' is taken from Bancha.

4.4 Japanese Tea by Region

Japan is a tea producing country, but some regions make more tea than others, and some are better known for a particular kind of tea.

Shizuoka prefecture is the largest producer of Japanese tea and accounts for around 40% of all Japanese tea. It is known for its deep steamed Sencha – **Fukamushicha**. Shizuoka mostly makes commodity tea, but some of the areas in the mountains such as Kawane and Tenryu make more premium teas.

Kagoshima prefecture on Kyushu island is the second largest Japanese tea producer, which makes about a third of all Japanese tea. It has been fortunate with the fertile soil due to an active nearby volcano. However, because of this, Kagoshima is also the only region that washes the tea leaves in the processing to remove the ashes.

Fukuoka prefecture is another tea region on Kyushu island. One of its areas – **Yame**, has recently gained fame for making premium Gyokuro and it is currently one of the biggest Gyokuro producers.

Kyoto prefecture is known for its long-time production of Japanese tea. In fact, it is popularly believed that some of the first tea seeds brought from China to Japan were planted in Kyoto. Its **Uji** area is famous both in Japan and around the world for premium Matcha and Gyokuro production.

Aichi prefecture is another tea growing region. Its **Nishio** area is known for Matcha and until recently it used to take the lead in the production of Matcha.

5   Chemical Composition of Tea

Tea and its properties have always instigated human curiosity. With the advancement of science, new methods to investigate the features and effects of tea became available. As we learn more of what is inside the tea leaf we can understand and explain the effects of it much better. This chapter will look into the nutrition of tea: what components are in the tea leaf and the effect they have. It will also explore the topic of contamination. Finally, it will look into how to store and preserve the good qualities of tea.

5.1   Tea Nutrition

In many cultures tea has been seen as an aid to one's health. In the early days, it was even used as medicine. Aided with the scientific research, today we know more about what components are in the tea leaf and the health benefits they can provide for us. In general, these components can be divided into water-soluble and non-soluble.

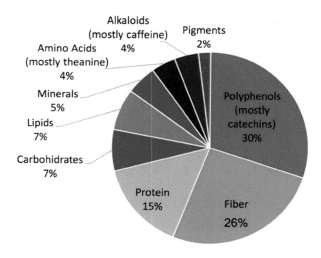

Chemical composition of green tea, data from Chacko S.M. et al. (2010)

Water-soluble components are these that you will find inside a cup of tea after tea leaves have been steeped in water. There are 4 key components in the water-soluble category: catechins, theanine, caffeine and vitamins.

Catechins are probably the most researched components of tea because of their antioxidant qualities. Catechins belong to the category of polyphenols (and a sub category of flavanols). If oxidized they turn into theaflavins and thearubigins[1], that bring dark color and bitter taste to oxidized tea. Catechins are derived from amino acids via sunlight[2] and account for about a third[3] of all the components in the tea leaf. They are known to bring astringent mouth-drying taste, which also serves as a natural defense mechanism whilst the plant is growing and helps to defer insects and diseases[4]. There are several kinds of catechins in a tea leaf, and the most abundant one is epigallocatechin (EGCG), that is ascribed to provide a number of health benefits. Catechins are said to lower the risk of heart diseases by reducing the absorption of bad cholesterol[5]. It is also known that catechins help to control the blood sugars and boost metabolism, which can reduce the risk of diabetes and aid in weight loss[6].

Theanine, scientifically called L-Theanine, is another important component of tea. It belongs to amino acid category, and amino acids are known to form proteins responsible for the metabolism and growth of an organism. Amino acids account for about 1-4% of a dry tea leaf weight[7]. Through exposure to sunlight theanine gets converted to catechins, so shading tea from the sun helps to retain a larger amount of theanine[8]. In tea it is responsible for a sweet and savory umami taste. It also has a calming and relaxing effect, as it tends to induce alpha waves in a brain[9], usually present during wakeful relaxation. The presence of theanine in tea stands to explain why historically tea has been used in Zen Buddhism and meditation.

Tea, like coffee, also has **caffeine**. It belongs to the category of alkaloids (and a sub category of methylxanthines). Alkaloids accounts for about 3-4% of a tea leaf weight[10]. New shoots and young tea leaves tend to have more caffeine than mature tea leaves[11]. Caffeine brings a bitter taste to the cup and because of that it has insect deterring qualities[12]. As we know, caffeine provides a stimulating effect. While in coffee it tends to instigate immediate energy spikes, in tea it works more slowly and gradually, as it interacts with theanine, that has a soothing quality. The combination of caffeine and theanine, thus, results in enhanced performance and focused attention[13]. Some Japanese teas made from young tea leaves, such as Matcha or spring Sencha, are rich in caffeine. Others made from more mature tea leaves, such as Bancha; or stems, such as Kukicha, will have much less of it.

Tea also contains vitamins, such as A, B, C, E. Among the vitamins, **vitamin C** is the most abundant. Vitamin C, like catechins, has an antioxidant quality - it is also an immunity booster.

In addition, to water-soluble components there are some components that do not dissolve in water. In fact, a tea leaf is largely made up of non-soluble components, such as fiber, protein, vitamins, minerals and pigments. Non-soluble fiber makes about a quarter of a tea leaf. When consumed it can help with digestion, as it aids the material movement through the digestive system. There are also a few vitamins that do not dissolve in water (but they do in fat). Such is vitamin A that aids the eyesight; and vitamin E, that protects skin and body tissue.

5.2   Tea Contamination

Tea is generally seen as a healthy product. However, with increasing tea consumption and focus on the health benefits of tea, some people have started to worry about tea contamination. Because of the environment where tea plants grow, as well as farming and processing techniques used, tea may get contaminated and acquire chemical ingredients that are foreign to its natural growth and development.

Recently the biggest concern is about pesticide residue in tea. As we have seen earlier, in modern farming pesticides are used to assist the tea plant in coping with pests and weeds. Currently there are several hundred registered chemicals that are the active components in the pesticides. After use, some of them easily break down in nature due to exposure to sunlight and rain. Others take much longer to break down and leave a residue on the tea leaves. Depending on the dosage some of the pesticides may have an adverse effect on our body and environment. However, the use of pesticides is strictly regulated and strict limits are set on how much residue can be allowed. Tea farmers in Japan tend to uphold the set standards. Therefore, even if pesticides are often used in Japan, the residues are usually within the set limits.

Another danger for contamination is from heavy metals, such as lead, cadmium, arsenic, etc. These metals tend to be present in environments with high industrial pollution. From the air they fall into the water and soil, from which they can be absorbed by a tea plant and brought into its leaves. High doses of heavy metals may lead to kidney, cardiovascular and neurological diseases[14]. As in the case of pesticides, however, there are strict residue levels for heavy metals and heavy metal contamination in Japanese tea is rarely a concern.

Lastly, because of the Fukushima accident in 2011, radioactive contamination has brought some concern. Tea leaves may be contaminated when exposed to radioactive components such as iodine, caesium, etc. Intake of these elements can increase the risk of cancer. Radioactive elements can travel through air, however the distance to the source is important and the areas within 80km of the accident place seem to have been affected the most[15].

5.3   Tea Preservation

Earlier in this chapter we talked about green tea nutrients. Some of them are more sensitive to the storing conditions and can get spoiled more easily. Key degrading factors for green tea nutrients and other components are: oxygen, heat, moisture, and light the exposure to which can lead to degradation[16].

Dangers to green tea

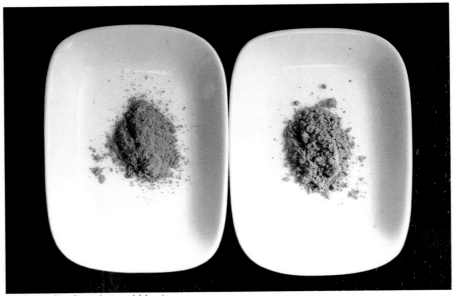

Well-stored and poorly-stored Matcha

Importance of filling up the container to the top

Japanese green tea is non-oxidized, which means that the tea contains antioxidants, that can still react with oxygen. Therefore, any exposure to air poses a risk to its quality. Green teas, hence, should be kept in air-tight containers to limit the exposure to the oxygen in the air. Air-tight, however, does mean air-free. It is recommended, therefore, to keep the container as full with tea leaves as possible to limit the amount of air that can get in. Some tea companies may even use oxygen absorbers, vacuum sealing or nitrogen flushing to remove the oxygen from the tea package.

Heat poses another danger, first of all because it can speed up oxidation, discussed above. In addition to this, some of the tea components, are sensitive to temperature, and can start breaking down if it reaches high enough points. Therefore, it is advisable to keep green tea refrigerated to slow down these chemical reactions in the tea leaf. Green tea, however, absorbs odor, so its aroma can be ruined if it is kept close to foods with a strong odor. In this case, same as above, having a tightly closed container is the key.

Moisture can also damage green tea. Processed tea usually retains around 5% moisture[17] and because of that it is quick to absorb moisture when exposed to it. Additional moisture in the package may induce a process similar to tea steeping, where flavors and aromas start to be released, spoiling the tea before you can even try it. Additionally, moisture may lead to the formation of molds, which would ruin the tea. Therefore, care is needed when tea is stored in a fridge because the difference between the temperature in a fridge and in the room, when the tea is taken out, can create condensation. To prevent the condensation, it is recommended to quickly take the needed amount of tea and immediately return the rest of it to the fridge.

Finally, light may also cause damage to tea. Quite a few nutrients, such as vitamins may degrade when exposed to light. Light also has a degrading effect on tea pigments, such as chlorophyll, the result of which will be the loss of the vivid green tea color[18]. To prevent this kind of degradation, it is recommended to avoid keeping the tea in clear containers, and instead to choose a non-see-though container that can keep the tea leaves away from the light.

If stored well and away from these dangers Japanese tea in its original package can last at least a year. The same storage rules still apply once the package is opened and depending on the kinds of tea it is usually recommended to finish the tea within a few months to enjoy it at its best.

6 Japanese Tea Brewing and Tasting

To enjoy Japanese tea flavors and aromas processed tea leaves first need to be steeped in water. There are several important factors and techniques that can determine the final result. This chapter will explore both tea brewing and tea tasting. It will first look into key parameters of tea brewing and then will explore some of the popular Japanese tea brewing techniques. After that, we will turn to tea tasting and will introduce both professional tea evaluation as well as a traditional blind tea tasting game. Finally, we will look at tea and food pairings which enable tea flavors to shine.

6.1   Tea Brewing Parameters

The taste of a Japanese tea can range from vegetal and sweet, to unbearably bitter depending on how you make it. Taste always relies on personal preference, but knowing the science behind it will help to make a good cup. There are a few key parameters to pay attention to when brewing Japanese green tea: water temperature, tea to water ratio, and steeping time as well as both tea and water quality.

Tea brewing parameters

Probably the most important parameter in tea brewing is water temperature, which will determine the extraction rate of water-soluble components. Some components, such as theanine, which is responsible for the umami taste (described as both savory-sweet and vegetably-brothy), are highly soluble and will have almost the same extraction rate regardless of temperature[1]. Others, such as catechins, that bring astringent bitterness to the cup, and caffeine, that also adds bitterness, depend on the temperature much more[2]. At higher temperature they will get extracted quickly, while at lower temperature they will have a much lower extraction rate. So changing the brewing temperature can change the taste profile of your tea: lower temperature will give a sweeter and more umami tea, whereas higher temperature will bring out more bitterness and astringency.

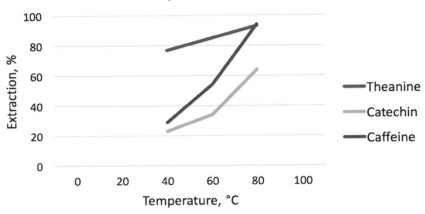

Green Tea Component Extraction into Water

Green tea component extraction into water, data from Ikeda S., at al. (1972)

Now, the strength of the tea will mostly be decided by the steeping time and tea to water ratio. Starting with the steeping time: Japanese tea is usually rather quick to release tea flavors into water – most of the time you don't need to go over a minute, and usually just 30 seconds can be enough. Steeping it less will make the tea taste weaker, steeping longer will turn it stronger.

The strength of the tea can also be adjusted with the tea to water ratio. In Japan teapots tend to be smaller in size than the western ones and would usually brew about 200ml – 300ml at a time. For that amount of water about 5g – 7g of tea are usually recommended. Using less tea leaves than that would make the brew lighter; and in contrast adding more tea leaves would make it more intense.

Finally, the end result of your cup of tea will also depend on the quality of tea and water. We know that tea leaves can vary in size: from full tea leaves to small tea segments. Small tea segments provide larger surface area for water to enter into the leaf, so they brew faster than full leaf teas. In addition to that, fresh tea will have many more taste components available compared to tea that has been kept for a while and may have lost some of the components to degradation[3].

Japanese black tea brewed with hard and soft water

Water quality is also immensely important, as water makes about 99% of your tea cup (only about 1% are soluble tea components)[4]. One of the key aspects in tea quality is whether water is soft or hard, which refers to the amount of minerals dissolved in it. The most common minerals that can be found in water are magnesium and calcium. Water with less than 100mg/l of minerals is classified as soft and water with more minerals than that is classified as hard[5]. Harder water tends to mask the taste and dull the color of tea, so for Japanese green tea soft water is recommended. In areas that have hard water you can either filter it to reduce the mineral content (charcoal filter recommended) or use bottled spring water. It is necessary to note that the aim for softer water does not mean completely removing all the minerals as that would lead to a dull and tasteless water and so a dull and ruined tea.

6.2   Tea Brewing Techniques for Japanese Tea

Most Japanese tea can be brewed several times – usually up to 3 or 4 times, depending on how strong you like it. Green tea is more sensitive to temperature as it has more catechins, that are extracted faster at a higher temperature[6]. So the most common way to brew Japanese green tea is to start with lower temperature and gradually increase it for the subsequent brews. For the first brew of high grade Japanese green tea water temperature between 50°C-60°C is usually recommended. The second brew would go higher to around 70°C-80°C and the final brew can be made with 90°C-100°C temperature. This way the tea taste is extracted gradually and provides a different experience with each cup: sweetness and umami at first, later more some bitterness and finally more astringency. It is also a good practice to pre-warm the teaware with hot water, which helps to keep the selected temperature for longer when steeping the tea.

47

Sencha brewed with warm water

In contrast to this, some recommend to steep Japanese tea with hot water (between 90℃-100℃) right away. Advocates of this brewing style argue that hot brews provide a more balanced taste of Japanese green tea, as it includes both umami and bitterness. In addition to this, it tends to bring out more of the aroma. One piece of advice, though, is to adjust the steeping time to just 20s-30s when making hot brews with Japanese green tea, as otherwise it can become really bitter and astringent.

Cold brew jug

Steeping tea with cold water is little known in the West, but it can provide an equally enjoyable tea. As we have learned before, cooler temperature lowers catechin extraction rate, so a cold brew (between 0℃-20℃) results in a sweeter tea with barely any bitterness at all. The suggested way is to add the tea leaves to a bigger jug or water bottle and keep it in a fridge for at least 1h-2h to extract enough flavor (overnight is also good).

6.3 Professional Tea Tasting

In addition to everyday tea tastings, there are also professional tea tastings, that are used to evaluate tea and determine which tea to select. In Japan professional tea tastings are quite different from casual tea tastings. They have defined tea evaluation criteria that usually involves the evaluation of the visual appearance of the dry tea leaves (shape and color), as well as aroma, color and taste of the brew. Commonly tea under evaluation has full points at the beginning; and points are subtracted for deviation from the ideal character of that kind of tea (and there are set standards for what an ideal tea should be)

Professional tea tasting

The shape and color of dry tea leaves can provide hints as to what kind of tea it is, how it has been farmed and what processing steps it has been through. For example, the size of the tea leaves can reveal the grade of the tea as well as the season it was made in. Smaller thinner tea leaves will hint to higher grade tea made in spring. Bigger flatter leaves will hint to lower grade tea and later harvesting seasons. In addition, longer leaves will tell that the tea was hand-picked, whereas shorter leaves will hint that the tea was machine harvested. Furthermore, fuller leaf segments will point to the tea being lightly steamed, whereas smaller leaf segments will hint to deep steaming. Stems in the tea mix will point that it is aracha.

Lightly steamed and deeply steamed tea

Steeped tea leaves may further confirm the assumptions above and reveal a few other aspects. For example, light green color of steeped leaves will show that the tea has been grown in full sunlight, whereas a dark green color tells that the tea was shaded before harvesting. And a mix of both would show that the tea was blended. In addition, full open tea leaves will reveal that the tea was harvested by hand; broken tea leaves, on the other hand, will show that the tea was harvested by machine.

Single origin tea and blended tea

After looking at the tea leaves, tea professionals can have a pretty good guess about the tea, even to such detail as the cultivar it is made from or the region it has been grown in. This will help them to manage their expectations, which will be tested in the next step – the evaluation of the brew.

The visual appearance of the brew will confirm if the tea is higher or lower quality. Higher grade tea made of the young shoots, will have dust-like baby tea hair (present only on the young tea leaves) on the surface of the liquor. Paler brew with a bluish tint will tell that the tea was shaded, whereas brew with a yellow tint will show that the tea was grown in the sun. The clear or cloudy brew will confirm if the tea was steamed lightly or deeply, respectively. Finally, the color of the brew can show if the tea has been kept well or not. Fresh and well-kept Japanese green teas will usually have a color ranging from green to light yellow. Darker yellow and orange tones may show that the tea was not stored well and may have oxidized.

Tea grown in the sun and in the shade

The aroma of the brew is checked next; and finally, its taste is assessed by swirling a sip of tea all around the mouth to expose the taste to as many taste buds as possible. With all of these observations in mind, the tea is then either discarded or selected for purchase.

6.4 Blind Tea Tasting – Chakabuki

資料茶

花	田辺玉露		4,000 円
鳥	両丹玉露		1,500 円
風	和束煎茶		1,500 円
月	桃香野冠茶		800 円
客	京都深蒸煎茶		600 円

List of teas for Chakabuki

In addition to casual and professional tea tastings and tea tastings – a tea tasting can take the form of a game. One such game is Chakabuki. It started as a fun pastime for the aristocracy centuries ago and now is often used to challenge tea professionals. Chakabuki is basically a blind tea tasting game and its participants get to comparatively taste 5 teas which have similar characteristics, such as Gyokuro, Kabuse Sencha and regular Sencha. First the participants learn which teas are included in the game and have a chance to look at the dry tea leaves of all 5 teas. That helps to create a mental image of all the teas and their characteristics. After that the teas are served one by one and judging tea color, aroma and taste, participants have to guess which tea it is. The game usually has 5 rounds, and the correct answers are given after each round, so that participants can learn their mistakes and adjust their guesses in the future. While it is a fun game, to do well, it requires an advanced palate, which is able to distinguish and identify different tastes and aromas.

6.5   Tea and Food Pairing

Of course, tea can be enjoyed on its own, but its taste can also be enhanced when paired with food. For centuries in Japanese tea ceremony as well as in everyday life tea has been paired with sweets to provide a more balanced experience. Nowadays tea pairing goes further to include both sweet and savory foods to either compliment or balance each other.

Matcha and sakura mochi

Japanese green teas are generally known for their light and vegetal flavor, so they perform better with foods that do not have strong overwhelming flavors. A common recommendation is to pair Japanese tea with fish, chicken, salad and fruit. Some of the Japanese teas also go well with cheese, chocolate and nuts.

More umami-rich and grassy teas such as Gyokuro or Kabuse Sencha can be paired to complement raw, steamed or lightly seasoned white fish.

Chicken, when boiled, steamed or grilled can be nicely accompanied by light and smooth Kukicha.

Some of lighter tasting cheeses such as brie, gouda, mozzarella (as well as cheese desserts), pair nicely with high grade Sencha.

Vegetable dishes (in a salad, steamed or grilled shape) that include cauliflower, broccoli, spinach, cabbage, corn, etc. can be complemented by rich and vegetal Matcha.

Chocolate with varying levels of cacao works really well with roasted tea –Hojicha, that helps to balance both potential sweetness and bitterness.

Finally, Genmaicha, that has roasted rice in its mix, goes to complement nutty savory and sweet recipes.

These are the general guidelines for Japanese tea and food pairings, though, and a specific combination will always depend on the individual preferences.

7 Japanese Tea History and Japanese Tea Today

Tea has been known to human kind for a long time. It is likely that first it was used for food. We do not know exactly when and how people started brewing tea, but a beautiful legend says, that it was a king in China – Shennong, into whose cup of water a tea leaf fell. Nonetheless, tea (especially Camellia Sinensis Sinensis variety) is said to have originated in China, from where it spread to the surrounding areas until it reached Japan.

Tea was first introduced to Japan by Buddhist monks. Then it changed and transformed through the centuries allowing Japan to develop its own tea practices and rituals. This chapter will delve into Japanese tea history. It will look into how tea was introduced to Japan, how it has transformed through time and what its current situation is.

7.1   The Beginning of Japanese Tea

It is commonly thought that tea was introduced to Japan by Japanese Buddhist monks, who went to China to study Buddhist teachings. On the way back they started bringing nuggets of Dancha (pressed brick tea that was common at that time) to their temples to aid Buddhist meditation. Slowly the habit of grinding the tea and dissolving it in hot water started to develop in Japan.

An image of Saicho, Y.Utagawa, Public domain

Then, at the beginning of 9th century, emperor Saga was invited to Bonshakuji temples (in Shiga prefecture), where he was served tea by Buddhist monk Eichu[1] – this is mentioned in Nihon Kouki (in English 'Later Chronical of Japan') and appears to be the earliest written record of tea drinking in Japan. Around the same time, two Buddhist monks Kukai and Saicho, who went on a mission to China, are said to have brought tea seeds to plant and grow them in Japan[2]. While tea consumption and cultivation was encouraged and supported by Emperor Saga[3], the habit was slow to catch on with the general public[4], and tea mostly remained within the confines of the temples.

An image of Eisai, Public domain

A few centuries had to pass until Eisai, another Buddhist monk and the founder of the largest Buddhist sect in Japan – Rinzai, went on to popularize Japanese tea. He was mainly interested in the medicinal properties of tea and wrote a book called 'Kissa Youjoki' (in English 'Drinking Tea for Health'). Like his predecessors Kukai and Saicho, Eisai also went on a few missions to China and brought tea seeds to Japan. It is said that these were planted in three locations: on a small island in Nagasaki prefecture, on Seburi Mountains in Saga prefecture and in Kozanji Temple north of Kyoto[5]. Later the tea was also planted in Uji, and became known as honcha – 'the real tea' (tea from other areas would be called hicha or 'non-tea')[6]. From there it spread throughout Japan.

The oldest tea field in Japan at Kozanji

7.2 Japanese Tea Through Time

The introduction of Japanese tea was not straightforward (it took several attempts), and neither were its later developments. As we have seen, after being brought to Japan tea remained mostly a temple activity for several centuries. Only after Eisai had tea seeds planted in several locations around Japan that tea cultivation, and tea consumption along with it, started to spread.

Gradually tea was adopted into the daily lives of the Japanese upper classes. Lavish tea parties to admire gorgeous Chinese tea utensils started to become a common pastime[7] and tea contests, requiring the participants to blindly taste and identify the real tea from Uji - honcha started to become popular[8]. At that time, tea gatherings were seen as an amusement and a pleasurable activity.

As time passed, however, a revolt against extravagance and luxury in tea enjoyment started to emerge. It invited to turn back to modesty and humbleness, and eventually resulted in the development of the Japanese tea ceremony that we know today.

In the 15th century the direction that the tea ceremony would take was first set by a Buddhist monk and a tea master - Murata Juko, and followed by a highly educated leather merchant and a tea master Takeno Joo, who then became the teacher for Sen no Rikyu – one of the most prominent figures in the history of Japanese tea ceremony.

Sen no Rikyu went on to formalize and standardize the enjoyment of tea in the 16th century. A new more modest way of tea started to become popular, and Sen no Rikyu became so influential, that even the military leaders of the time, such as Oda Nobunaga and, after his death, Toyotomi Hideyoshi, came to rely on him. Until eventually Sen no Rikyu was condemned to death by suicide for reasons unknown to this day.

An image of Sen no Rikyu, H.Touhaku, Public domain

Tokugawa Ieyasu, the successor of the Toyotomi Hideyoshi, eventually unified Japan under Tokugawa Shogunate in 1600 and brought a long-lasting period of peace. Militancy lost its prominence and tea came to provide a scene for social networking and information gathering[9].

As time passed, literati and artistic echelons of Japanese society started to feel disappointed by the rigidness of the tea ceremony[10]. In search for alternatives, they turned once again to China, where loose leaf tea had already replaced powdered tea.

Ingen – a Buddhist monk from China and the founder of the Obaku Buddhist sect in Uji, was the one who brought loose leaf tea (later to be known as Sencha) to Japan in 17th century[11]. Sencha culture then spread around Japan due to a Buddhist monk from Obaku sect – Baisao, who travelled around Kyoto and wider Japan selling Sencha with his mobile tea stall (Graham P., 2001)[12].

An image of Baisao, Public domain

During Sakoku – Japan's closure from the outside world between 1635–1854 – trade with China and other countries became limited. This restricted access to Chinese loose-leaf tea and gave Japan an opportunity to create local tea production methods.

In the 18th century Nagatani Souen, a tea maker in Kyoto invented a new way of processing tea[13] and essentially created a loose-leaf tea, unique to Japan – Sencha. As the production of Sencha spread and its consumption spilled over across the different layers of Japanese society, it soon became the most common type of tea.

Matcha and the traditional tea ceremony, on the other hand, continued mostly in the hands of the elites. With the end of Sakoku demanded by the US, Japan realized that it was behind the western world and needed to catch up. This led to Meiji restoration (return of power from the military leader to the emperor) and a rapid industrialization in Japan at the end of 19th century. To legitimize their power, the newly created wealthy class of industrialists and big company owners went in search of a connection with the past and they found their answer in tea ceremony[14].

Once the position of the new industrialists was established, tea ceremony was passed on to women. In the early 20th century knowledge of tea ceremony and other traditional Japanese arts was deemed desirable in a potential wife, and so the practice of tea ceremony became widespread among women[15].

Later on tea ceremony somewhat lost its prominence, with only a small fraction of active practitioners today. Nonetheless, it has become the cultural symbol of Japan and has been receiving a growing international interest.

7.3 Japanese Tea Today

Currently Japan ranks No.8 in world tea production and accounts for about 2% world tea[16]. Sencha makes up about two thirds of Japanese tea. Bancha comes second with around 20%. Matcha, even if growing in popularity in Japan and around the world, accounts for only about 2%[17].

The largest tea producing area is Shizuoka prefecture, which makes around 40% of Japanese tea; Kagoshima comes second with around 30%[18]. These two prefectures together make more than two thirds of Japanese tea. Other tea producing prefectures are much smaller in proportion. For example, Kyoto makes only about 3% of Japanese tea[19].

Thanks to improvements in technology as well as in farming and processing techniques the production amount of Japanese tea continued to grow through most of 20th century (except the times of war and other crises). Tea production amount peaked in late 1970s[20], when Japan experience rapid economic grow. Since mid 2000s, however, it has been in decline.

A few factors may lend some explanation. One is the decreasing domestic demand for Japanese tea. Japanese population is shrinking in general and young people are turning away from Japanese tea, that is seen as old-fashioned and something of the past century, to something new and more exciting like black tea or coffee. Consequently, the decrease in domestic demand is accompanied by the decline in the market price for Japanese tea (especially since early 2000s)[21].

Declining demand is also met with declining supply. Japan has the known issue of an aging population, and agriculture seems to be one of the most affected sectors. In some traditional tea farming towns most of the tea farmer population is in their 60s and 70s, who will inevitably retire, and there are only a few younger farmers willing to take over.

Growing international interest in Japanese tea, on the other hand, may offer some resolution to the declining Japanese tea industry. The export amount of Japanese tea has grown considerably over the last 20 years; and currently about 5% of Japanese tea is exported aboard[22]. Mayor importers of Japanese tea are US, Taiwan, Singapore, Germany and Canada[23]. However, because the exported amount of Japanese tea remains relatively small, it may take years or even decades until tea exports can make a more significant impact in reenergizing Japanese tea industry.

World Tea Production by Country

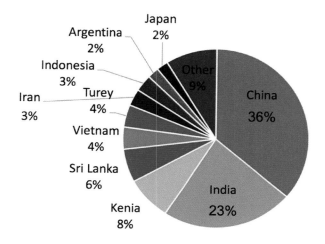

World tea production by country, data from Chang K (2015)

Japanese Tea Production by Kind

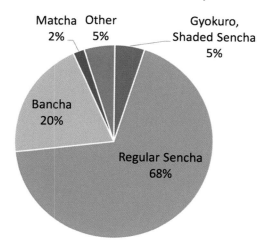

Japanese tea production by kind, data from Japanese Tea Instructors Association (2015)

Main Tea Producing Regions in Japan

5. Kyoto

6. Fukuoka

8. Saga

9. Kumamoto

1. Shizuoka

10. Aichi

3. Mie

7. Nara

4. Miyazaki

2. Kagoshima

Main tea producing regions in Japan, data from Japanese Tea Instructors Association (2015), map outline from http://d-maps.com/carte.php?num_car=24833&lang=en

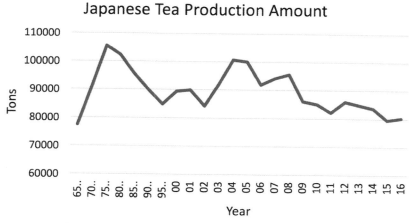

Japanese tea production amount, data from Japanese Ministry of Agriculture, Forestry and Fisheries

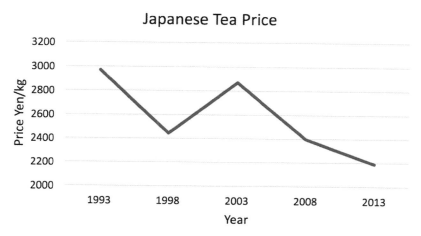

Price of spring Sencha, data from Japanese Tea Instructors Association (2015)

8 The Japanese Tea Ceremony

The Japanese tea ceremony, sometimes called 'the way of tea' to convey a broader meaning, started to develop several centuries ago. It has continued to transform through time and today it is seen as a cultural symbol of Japan. This chapter will explore the beginnings of the tea ceremony, and will introduce the philosophies guiding the practice. It will then touch on ritual of the ceremony and will introduce different schools that practice and teach the way of tea. Lastly a different and less known kind of tea ceremony – Senchado – will be addressed.

8.1   The Beginnings of the Tea Ceremony

The formation of the tea ceremony was a gradual process that took several hundred years. It began mostly as an enjoyable gathering of the wealthy; then in 15th century it developed some deeper concepts and defining practices and finally gained a more structured form in the 16th century.

An image of Murata Juko, Public domain

The beginning of the tea ceremony formation is attributed to Murata Juko (sometimes spelled as Murata Shuko) - a Zen Buddhist monk, and later a renowned tea master. He is said to have instigated the rustic style of tea by bringing tea gatherings to a rustic hut and combining simple modest Japanese teaware – wamono, with fancy Chinese teaware – karamono[1]. Murata Juko also raised tea ceremony to a more spiritual level and gave it its first defining values: reverence, respect, purity and tranquility[2]. In the physical world, he set the tearoom size to four and a half tatami mats for smaller and more serene tea gatherings.

A statue of Takeno Joo, Public domain

After Murata Juko, the development of tea continued by Takeno Joo, a tea master with a high education in poetry and other arts. He studied under a Murata Juko's student and carried his work forward. Takeno Joo's greatest contribution to the tea ceremony is the introduction of wabi – 'an aesthetic affirmation of insufficiency'[3]. It is also believed that Takeno Joo has brought about the concept of 'Ichi Go Ichi E (in English 'one life one chance') to tea[4].

An image of Sen no Rikyu, H.Touhaku, Public domain

From Takeno Joo, the work of wabi-cha was taken over by his student Sen no Rikyu, who became a renowned tea master and an influential figure in political life. He standardized the tea ceremony practice and gave the seven precepts for the tea ceremony students to follow. After Sen no Rikyu, his teachings were mainly passed through his family line and survived until today in three main schools of the tea ceremony.

8.2   The Philosophy of the Tea Ceremony

Since the introduction of tea form China to Japan, Japanese tea has developed in a close connection with Zen Buddhism. At first tea was brought to Japan by Japanese Buddhist monks, and later tea masters, who gave the beginning to the development of the tea ceremony, such as Murata Juko, Takeno Joo and Sen no Rikyu, also studied Zen. The philosophy of the tea ceremony, therefore, has also been greatly influenced by it.

Inspired by Zen Buddhism, at the center of the tea ceremony is the concept of **wabi**. Having originally referred to despair and loneliness[5], the meaning of wabi transformed through time to refer to honesty, humbleness and modesty[6]. Because of wabi, aesthetically insufficiency came to be appreciated. Even before the concept of wabi was introduced to tea, Murata Juko already leaned to the impression of 'chill and withered' in tea[7]. Takeno Joo took it a step further and saw wabi as providing desolate and bare impression in tea[8]. Hence, in those times, simple and rustic Japanese teaware started to be chosen over fancy Chinese teaware; gorgeous wide tea spaces gave way to small and modest tearooms.

In addition to that, 'Ichi Go Ichi E', taught by Takeno Joo[9], became an important concept in tea. It means 'one life one chance' and urges tea ceremony participants to cherish every single moment, as no tea gathering will be repeated in the exact same manner again.

Ichi Go Ichi E

Tea ceremony is also guided by four core values (first introduced by Murata Juko and later revised by Sen no Rikyu[10]): harmony, respect, purity and tranquility (in Japanese 'Wa Kei Sei Jaku').

Wa Kei Sei Jaku

Harmony refers to being at peace with the people and nature. More practically it means being considerate to one another and sensitive to the changes in the nature, and is reflected in the choice of the utensils and the setup of the tearoom.

Another core value – **respect** – is expected from everyone involved in a tea gathering, including both the host and guests. Without one or the other tea gathering would not be possible. So a mutual respect is needed for a successful enactment of the ceremony; and it results in a polite and considerate treatment of each other.

Purity refers to cleanliness in both the physical and spiritual worlds. Simple tasks of cleaning the space and purifying the utensils in the physical world also help to cleanse the spirit and prepare the heart for the tea gathering.

Tranquility means the ultimate serenity and peace, in other cultures referred to as enlightenment or nirvana. It may be hard to achieve it directly, and the way to it is through constant observation of the first three values.

In addition to these four values, Sen no Rikyu added a few more rules for the students of the tea ceremony to follow. Today they are known as the seven precepts of Sen no Rikyu[11], that help to guide the practice of the ceremony:

The first is to make a delicious bowl of tea. No further directions are given, and that hints to the serving of tea being less about the techniques of making tea and more about the sincerity and hospitality of the host.

The second is to lay charcoal for water to boil. Back in the old days water used to be heated over burning charcoal. Hence, the arrangement of charcoal was very important to ensure that the water was ready for tea when needed. Even today charcoal arrangements in front of the guests remains a part of the traditional tea ceremony.

The third is to arrange flowers like they are in nature. It stresses the importance of being in harmony with nature. Even if flowers are borrowed from the field, to cherish their life they need to be displayed as if they are in nature.

The forth is to provide a sense of coolness in summer and warmth in winter. Nature has its own rhythm, which gives us summers and winters. Fortunately, there are many ways to warm up in winter and cool down in summer, such as using a sunken hearth for the kettle in winter to keep the heat longer and serving tea in wider more open tea bowls in summer to cool it down faster.

The fifth is to be ready ahead of time. It suggests cherishing the time as a precious resource. In the tea ceremony, the host needs to be ready before the guests arrive, and in appreciation of the host's effort the guests should also be there on time.

The sixth is to be prepared in case it might rain. In the old days, forecasting rain was much more difficult, so everyone had to be prepared for the rain all the time. These days it is understood as a metaphor that means to be prepared for the unexpected. During the tea ceremony the host may trip, the items may fall down, etc., but it is important to remain calm and react with composure.

The seventh is to be considerate of those around you. It draws on the importance of mutual respect and may involve expressing gratitude to the host for making tea or apologizing to the other guests for going first.

Engaging in the philosophy of tea ceremony makes you realize that tea ceremony is more than a technical ritual or an aesthetically pleasing performance. It is based on some deep underlying concepts that are important within and outside the practice of the tea ceremony. For this reason, some dislike the English term – tea ceremony; and instead choose to call it 'the way of tea'; to convey a broader meaning.

8.3   The Flow of the Tea Ceremony

Tea ceremony can be classified into formal and informal events. Informal tea ceremony, called chakai, can be held more freely and may involve serving a bowl of tea with some sweets. A formal tea ceremony, called chaji, on the other hand, is a much longer and more complicated event, that involves a meal, appreciation of the art and eventually serving of two kinds of tea. There are many different variations of chaji depending on the season, time of the day and occasion. Below is the description of one of the most common flows.

When the guests arrive for chaji, they are served a welcome drink in the waiting room. It is during the welcome drink that the guests decide the order of how they will sit in the tearoom. The first guest, called shoukyaku, has the most important role as he/she will lead the conversation with the host and will give an example to the other guests.

Once the order is decided, one by one guests proceed to the water fountain in the garden, called tsukubai, where they purify themselves by washing their hands and rinsing their mouths. After the purification is complete, in the same order as before guests enter the tearoom and head to the alcove at the front of the tearoom, called tokonoma, where kakejiku - the scroll of the day is displayed. After viewing the scroll, guests take their corresponding seats and wait for the host.

Tsukubai – a water fountain

Teishu – the host then enters the tearoom and performs the shozumi - charcoal arrangement. The water for the tea is heated by burning charcoal, so it is important to arrange it correctly to make sure the water boils on time, and hence the arrangement is performed in front of the guests.

Teishu – the host, by A.Poian

69

After this, guests are served a meal, called kaiseki, which involves several traditional dishes accompanied by Japanese sake and at the end Japanese sweets – wagashi. The meal is followed by a break during which the guests wait in the garden as the host rearranges the room and replaces the scroll in the alcove with the flower arrangement of the day.

Wagashi – Japanese sweets

Once the preparations are finished the host calls the guests back with a bell or gong. Then one by one guests return to the tearoom to view the flower arrangement before taking their seats again.

The host then enters the tearoom bringing and laying out utensils needed for the first serving of tea. Koicha, or thick tea, that resembles a green paste rather than a drink, is served. Before making and serving the tea the host carefully cleanses the utensils in front of the guests. The prepared bowl of tea is then served to the first guest and shared among all the guests by each of them taking three sips and wiping the edge of the bowl before passing it along. When the guests finish the tea, the host cleanses the utensils once again and passes them to the first guest for viewing, who later passes them on to the other guests.

After the thick tea, the host performs gozumi – the rearrangement of the charcoal to ensure good continuation of the fire. This marks the change from the formal to a more casual event. After that another round of sweets is brought and placed in front of the first guest. Following that, the host brings and lays out new utensils needed for the next tea. Like before the utensils are cleansed before preparing the tea. This time it is a thin tea, called Usucha, that is whisked with a bamboo whisk to create a smooth foam on the surface of the tea. The tea is served to the first guest, and the other guests receive their individual bowls afterwards.

Usucha - thin tea

After all the guest have finished their tea, the host will cleanse the utensils again and will provide them for viewing. The host then collects the utensils and leaves the tearoom. That marks the end of the ceremony and guests are free to leave.

The roles of both the host and the guest are important to ensure a smooth event. Both roles will usually require some training to understand how the event will unfold and how everyone needs to behave. For those with little experience, tea ceremony may appear rigid and stiff, but learning the routines helps to ensure that everyone knows the flow and can feel at ease during the event.

8.4   The Setup of the Tea Ceremony

The Japanese Tea Ceremony is held in a Japanese-style tearoom. The traditional size is four and a half tatami mats, but nowadays it can range from four and a half to ten or more tatami mats. A traditional tearoom usually has an alcove at the front of the room, called tokonoma, for displaying the scroll and flower arrangement. It also has entrances for the host and the guests. Traditionally the guest entrance was a 'crawl-in entrance' called nishiiriguchi, that made guests lower and humble themselves before entering. Today a regular sliding door entrance is also common. In addition to that, a traditional tea room usually has a sunken hearth for the kettle that will be open in the winter and closed in the summer.

The utensils will be selected and laid out specifically for each event. They will normally include a tea bowl, a tea caddy, a Matcha scoop, a Matcha whisk, a water kettle, a ladle for scooping water, etc. (which will be introduced in more detail in the next chapter).

While tea ceremony involves a lot of items, they are not picked randomly and usually correspond to a unifying theme of the event. It may be highlighting a particular time of the year or focusing on a particular artist, etc. It is also common that utensils are in contrast with one another (such as round and square, single-colored and multicolored etc.) to highlight the uniqueness of each and reflect on the yin and yang nature of all creations.

8.5   Tea Ceremony Schools

Today, tea ceremony is taught by several tea schools. Most of them tend to uphold the general concepts of tea philosophy and usually may only differ in the practical execution.

There are three traditional schools known as Sansenke, namely Urasenke, Omotesenke, and Mushanokojisenke. Senke translated from Japanese means the 'house of Sen' and all three claim their start and continuation through the Sen no Rikyu bloodline. They were founded by Sen no Rikyu's great grandchildren and passed from one generation to another mostly through a blood connection[12]. Interestingly enough the headquarters of all three are in Kyoto, housed in a close vicinity of each other. Urasenke tea school appears the biggest and most influential with about 70% tea practitioners in Japan today; Omotesenke come second with about 20%[13].

Aside from Sansenke, throughout Japan there are about a dozen of other schools that teach tea ceremony[14] and most of them started independently from Sansenke. They are usually much smaller in size than Sansenke schools and tend to be based more locally. A few more prominent examples are Oribe ryu, started in the 16th century by Furuta Oribe – the student of Sen no Rikyu; and Enshu ryu, started in the 17th century by Kobori Enshu – the student of Furuta Oribe. In contrast to the merchant origins of Sansenke schools, both teach warrior style ceremony; and Enshu ryu places kirei-sabi, or elegant simplicity, at its center[15].

8.6   Senchado

Everything discussed in this chapter so far, refers to traditional tea ceremony, which uses Matcha, and is called Chado. However, this is not the only kind of tea ceremony in Japan. There is also a ceremony involving Sencha - Senchado.

As described in the history chapter Sencha was introduced to Japan as an alternative to a too formal and rigid Chado. As Sencha provided more flexibility for expression and enjoinment, it was appreciated by Japanese artists and literati[16]. These literati also admired Chinese culture, and this had a significant influence on the development of Senchado. Unlike Chado, Senchado disregarded wabi style, and turned to appreciate the beauty of the refined Chinese style instead. This resulted in Senchado being much brighter and more colorful. Red and gold – common Chinese colors – are often present in Sencha ceremony.

Senchado at Ogasawara Sencha Service School, by K.Alyono

As time passed, however, Senchado became standardized and formalized too[17]. As with Chado it now has certain rules and routines to follow. However, while Sencha is the most produced tea in Japan, Senchado remains little known and there are only a few people who actively practice it today.

9 Japanese Teaware

The enjoyment of tea is impossible without teaware. And without tea, teaware loses its meaning, so tea and teaware are highly interconnected. At the beginning when tea was brought to Japan from China, Chinese teaware travelled along with it. Later Japanese pottery artists started making teaware domestically, and several distinct Japanese pottery styles developed. This chapter will briefly look at the history of Japanese teaware. It will also introduce key pottery styles and main teaware items.

9.1 The History of Japanese Teaware

Open fire pit

Pottery already existed in Japan before tea culture began. Some of the pottery items, made in open fire pits, that have survived to this day, date beck well before the current era. Roofed anagama kilns start to appear around the 5th century[1], leading to the development of Sue pottery, characterized by its dark grey color. It continued for several centuries and gradually declined, giving space for the development of new pottery styles. From around 7th-8th century Japanese pottery started to diversify. Among the first styles to appear were Tokonameyaki in Aichi prefecture, Skigarakiyaki in Shiga prefecture as well as Bizenyaki in Okayama prefecture (Yaki means pottery in Japanese). They are also included in the list of the six most noteworthy traditional kilns in Japan.

Anagama kiln

The move away from Chinese teaware during the standardization of the tea ceremony in the 16th century gave a new impetus to the development of Japanese teaware. It advanced further when Korean potters were brought to Japan after Japan's invasion at the end of 16th century[2]. These potters helped to make technological improvements in Japanese kilns and were instrumental in the start of Japanese porcelain production (especially for Aritayaki style from Saga prefecture). Today there are over a hundred pottery sites across Japan.

Clay is the most predominant material in Japanese teaware. However, other kinds of materials, such as bamboo, lacquer, iron, etc., are used for specific tea ware items. Commonly, their development went alongside the development of the tea ceremony.

9.2   Main Pottery Styles and Regions

Different kinds of teaware have been produced all over Japan. Some areas, though, came to be known more as they developed more distinct styles. Areas with the most recognized pottery styles include Kyoto, Mie, Shiga, Aichi, Gifu, Fukui, Okayama and Yamaguchi on the Honshu island of Japan, as well as Saga on the Kyushu island of Japan.

Different kinds of teaware have been produced all over Japan. Some areas, though, came to be known more as they developed more distinct styles. Areas with the most recognized pottery styles include Kyoto, Mie, Shiga, Aichi, Gifu, Fukui Okayama and Yamaguchi on the Honshu island of Japan, as well as Saga on the Kyushu island of Japan.

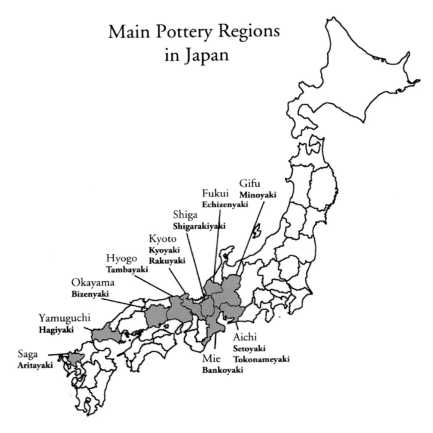

Main Pottery Regions in Japan

Gifu
Minoyaki

Fukui
Echizenyaki

Shiga
Shigarakiyaki

Kyoto
Kyoyaki
Rakuyaki

Hyogo
Tambayaki

Okayama
Bizenyaki

Yamuguchi
Hagiyaki

Aichi
Setoyaki
Tokonameyaki

Mie
Bankoyaki

Saga
Aritayaki

Main pottery regions in Japan, map outline from http://d-maps.com/carte.php?num_car=24833&lang=en

76

Going from the north of Japan to the south, **Tokonameyaki** from Aichi prefecture is one of the oldest pottery styles, dating back to the 12th century[3]. It is known for using iron-rich clay, which results in the vibrant red color of its wares. In terms of teaware, presently Tokonameyaki mainly produces Sencha utensils such as kyusu and accompanying cups.

Tokonameyaki kyusu

Setoyaki is another pottery style with a long history from Aichi prefecture. Its new glazed celadon wares became so popular, that all teaware in Japan were referred to as "Setomono"[4] (translated to English this means "Seto item"). Today Seto continues to produce Matcha utensils and is recognized for its beautiful combination of green brown and white colors.

Another old pottery style – **Shigarakiyaki** from Shiga prefecture is said to have started around 13th century[5] Shigarakiyaki is recognized for its earthy colors and rough texture of its mostly undecorated wares. It is also known for its clay raccoons – symbol of good fortune, which are often placed at the entrance to restaurants and bars in Japan. In terms of teaware, Shigaraki has been known for water vessels and vases used in tea ceremony.

Shigarakiyaki chawan

Bankoyaki kyusu

Bankoyaki in the neighboring Mie prefecture is a more recent style. It uses iron rich soil, but because of a special firing technique that limits the supply of oxygen, the result is dark purple teaware. Today Bankoyaki is mostly known for Kyusu and accompanying cups.

Kyoyaki chawan

Kyoyaki is a pottery style form Kyoto that started around the 17th century[6]. It has developed in a close connection with the tea ceremony, and hence the main focus in the area has been on producing tea ceremony utensils such as tea bowls and tea caddies. Kyoyaki is recognized for ivory-color glaze and vivid decorations.

Rakuyaki chawan

Another pottery style in Kyoto – **Rakuyaki** is also more recent in history dating back to the 16th century[7]. Rakuyaki started, when a roof-tile maker was tasked by Sen no Rikyu to make a tea bowl; and developed in a close connection with the tea ceremony. Today Rakuyaki is mostly known for its black- or red-glazed tea bowls[8]. Raku wares are fired at lower temperatures than other pottery styles, hence, items are more delicate and fragile.

Bizenyaki in Okayama prefecture is one of the old traditional pottery styles, that has started around the 12th century. Similar to Shigarakiyaki (that is said to have been influenced by Bizen potters) it is recognized by earthy colors and rough texture. In terms of teaware, it is known for water vessels and vases used in tea ceremony.

Bizenyaki chawan

Hagiyaki is a pottery style from Yamaguchi prefecture, which historically has been influenced by Korean potters brought to Japan[9] after Japan's invasion in Korea at the end of 16th century. It is mostly known for its tea bowls and recognized for natural pinkish color and dripping white glaze.

Hagiyaki chawan

In terms of porcelain (clay fired at really high temperatures), Japan is mostly known for **Aritayaki** from Saga prefecture. Clay suitable for porcelain was discovered by Korean potters brought to Japan after Japan's invasion in Korea at the end of 16th century[10]. Soon after that Aritayaki came to lead Japan's porcelain production. Aritayaki style includes a wide range of items and you can find some teacups too.

9.3 Main Japanese Teaware Items

Japanese teaware can be divided into utensils used for Matcha and utensils used for Sencha. The utensils used for Matcha have been briefly introduced in the previous chapter and will be explained below. Utensils for Sencha will follow after that.

Among the Matcha utensils first and foremost is a tea bowl, called **chawan**, which is used for making and serving tea. Some particular pottery styles such as Rakuyaki and Hagiyaki are more common in tea ceremony, but the bowls may vary greatly in shape, color and decoration. For example, wider more open tea bowls are used in summer to let the tea cool faster and in turn winter tea bowls have their edges raised up much more to keep the heat of the tea. In addition, tea bowls used for koicha usually have more muted colors and no decorations, whereas tea bowls for usucha tend to be brighter and more colorful.

Winter chawan and summer chawan

Natsume and chaire

In addition, for the tea ceremony Matcha is placed in a tea caddy and there are two different types depending if it is a thick or thin tea being prepared. For thin tea, Matcha is placed into a lacquer caddy called **natsume** and for thick tea a ceramic caddy, called **chaire**, is used.

Chashaku and chasen

A bamboo whisk called **chasen** is also necessary for whisking tea. It is usually made form a single piece of bamboo split into eighty finely carved parts. **Chashaku** – a bent bamboo scoop is used for measuring tea into the bowl.

Chagama

Another item necessary for tea ceremony is an iron kettle, called **chagama**, which is placed over charcoal to heat water for the tea ceremony. In addition to that, **hishaku** – a bamboo ladle – is used to scoop water from the kettle into the tea bowl.

Mizusashi and kensui

The traditional layout for the tea ceremony also usually has a **mizusashi** – a water container for refilling the kettle; and **kensui** – a utensil for dumping the used water.

Fukusa

Finally, every host will carry a silk cloth, called **fukusa**, for wiping and purifying the utensils. And a white cloth, called **chakin**, will usually be placed in a tea bowl for wiping it after rinsing with water.

Items needed for brewing Sencha are completely different. In the most simple and casual way Sencha can be made only with a teapot and some tea cups. As pottery making evolved through time, a few different kinds of teapots developed.

Kyusu

Kyusu is the most-well known and most commonly used Japanese teapot. Its characteristic feature is a handle at a 90-degree angle with the spout. In addition to that, it usually has a filter inside to separate the brew from the tea leaves when pouring it out. The filter can be made by poking holes directly in the wall of the teapot or by adding a metal mesh inside, where the spout meets the body of the pot.

Houhin

Houhin is another kind of Japanese teapot. It is said to be a generation older than a kyusu, because it does not have a handle. It is also usually smaller in capacity and made from porcelain. Houhin is often recommended for higher grade teas, such as Gyokuro or Kabuse Sencha.

83

Shiboridashi

Shiboridashi is yet another kind of Japanese teapot, that is thought to have come before the houhin. Hence, unlike houhin, it does not even have a filter and its spout is much smaller. The area around the spout inside the teapot has a few deep ridges carved into the clay, which works as a rudimentary filter, holding the tea leaves in and allowing the liquid out.

Yuzamashi

A utensil unique to Sencha brewing is a water cooler, called **yuzamashi**. In essence yuzamahi is a small bowl with a spout-like opening, and sometimes a handle on the side. Yuzamashi is used to cool the water for tea by moving the water back and forth between the yuzamashi and the teapot. Yuzamashi may also be used to hold excess water or to serve the brewed tea to distribute its taste more evenly to the guests.

Yunomi

Lastly is the tea cup – called **yunomi**. Japanese tea cups come in all shapes and colors, but they tend to be smaller in capacity than the western cups. Some high-grade teas, such as Gyokuro or Kabuse Sencha require even smaller cups, which allow a slower appreciation of the tea

.

84

10 Conclusion

Japan has a rich tea culture with long-lasting traditions. Tea has grown here for more than 800 years after it was brought from China by Buddhist monks. Through time Japanese tea has developed its own rituals and ceremonies. Later technological improvements in farming and processing helped to make it accessible to the general public.

Recently, however, domestic popularity of Japanese tea has been declining – it is now seen as old-fashioned and something of the past century. Few households still have a Kyusu for making tea and purchasing bottled tea from vending machines has become more common.

Decreasing domestic popularity of Japanese tea, on the other hand, is met with a growing interest abroad, due to a strong focus on health and healthy lifestyles. Japanese green tea, and Matcha especially, have come to be valued for their health properties.

The export of Japanese tea abroad, however, remains just around 5%, so international curiosity may not make a strong impact year. Decline in the domestic Japanese tea market, nonetheless, encourages to look abroad.

More effort, both domestically and internationally, hence, is necessary to keep Japanese tea and its wonderful culture going. Even a reader of this Guide like yourself can contribute to it by maintaining curiosity about Japanese tea and continuing to appreciate it. Every cup counts!

Notes

Chapter 2

1 For more details look at Banerjee, B. (1992), pp.25-53

2 For more details look at Japanese Tea Instructors Association (2015), pp.61-132 (in Japanese)

3 For more details look at Othieno, C.O. (1992), pp.137-173

4 For more details look at Okano, K., et al. (1997), pp.279-287

5 More at Japanese Tea Instructors Association (2015), pp.61-132 (in Japanese)

6 For more details look at Deng W.W., et al. (2008), pp.115‑119

7 More at Chu D.C., et.al. (1997), pp:129-137

8 Look at IFOAM (2017). *Definition of Organic Agriculture*. [online] Available at: https://www.ifoam.bio/en/organic-landmarks/definition-organic-agriculture Accessed on 2017.08.05

9 Look at OFRF. *Organic FAQs*. [online] Available at: http://ofrf.org/organic-faqs Accessed on 2017.08.06

10 For more details look at Kirchmann H. et al. (2008), pp.38-73

11 For more details look at Kristiansen P., Acram T. et al. (2006), pp.421-443

12 Look at IFOAM (2014). *Organic Japan and the Global Organic Network*. Available at http://www.ifoam.bio/sites/default/files/organics_in_japan.pdf [online] Accessed on 2017.08.06

13 Look at JONA (2017). *JONA Organic Standards 2017*. [online] Available at http://www.jona-japan.org/form/JONA_Standards.pdf Accessed on 2017.08.07

Chapter 3

1 Look at Japanese Tea Instructors Association (2013), pp.51-70 (in Japanese)

2 Look at (Japanese Tea Instructors Association (2015), pp.133-189 (in Japanese)

3 Look at Japanese Tea Instructors Association (2013), pp.51-70 (in Japanese)

4 Look at Japanese Tea Instructors Association (2013), pp.143-172 (in Japanese)

Chapter 4

1 Look at Japanese Tea Instructors Association (2013), pp.143-172 (in Japanese)

2 Look at Tanihata A. (1984), pp7-27

Chapter 5

1 Look at Varnam A. and Sutherland J.M. (1994), pp.171-190

2 Look at Voung Q.V., et al. (2011), pp.1931-1939

3 Look at Chacko S.M., et al. (2010), pp.1-13

4 Look at Friedman M. (2007), pp.116-134

5 For more look at Velayutham P., et al. (2008), pp.1840-1850

6 For more look at Wolfram S. (2007), pp.373S-388S

7 Look at Chacko S.M., et al (2010), pp.1-13

8 Look at Voung Q.V., et al. (2011), pp.1931-1939

9 Look at Voung Q.V., et al. (2011), pp.82-90

10 Look at Chacko S.M., et al. (2010), pp.1-13

11 Look at Lin Y.S., et al. (2003), pp1864-1873

12 Look at Monhanpuria P., et al. (2010), pp.275-287

13 Look at Bryan J. (2008), pp.82-90

14 Look at Jarup L. (2003), pp.167-182

15 Look at Yasunari T.J., at al. (2011), pp 19530-19534

16 For more look at Robertson G.L (1998), pp.588-621

17 For more look at Japanese Tea Instructors Association (2013), pp.51-70 (in Japanese)

18 Look at Ostalova M., et al. (2014), pp.S103-S109

Chapter 6

1 Look at Ikeda S., Nakagawa M. et al. (1972), pp.69-78 (in Japanese)

2 Look at Ikeda S., et al. (1972), pp.69-78 (in Japanese)

3 For more look at Friedman M., Lewin C.E., et al. (2008), pp. H47-H51

4 Look at Battle, V. (2017), pp.75-84

5 Look at Pani B. (2007), pp.277-278

6 Look at Ikeda S., et al. (1972), pp.69-78 (in Japanese)

Chapter 7

1 For more look at Genshitsu S. et al. (2011), pp.3-32

2 Look at Mair V.H., et al. (2009), pp. 84-93

3 Look at Murai Y. (1989), pp.3-32

4 Look at Munsterberg H. (2010), pp.32-55

5 Look at Mair V.H., et al (2009), pp.85-94

6 Look at Mair V.H., et al. (2009), pp.85-94

7 Look at Surak K. (2013), pp.57-90

8 For more look at Mair V.H., et al. (2009), pp.85-94

9 For more look at Surak K. (2013). pp.57-90

10 For more look at Graham P. (2001), pp.137-166

11 For more look at Graham P. (2003), pp.110-136

12 For more look at Graham P. (2001), pp.65-98

13 Look at Graham P. (2001), pp.137-166

14 Look at Surak K. (2013), pp.57-90

15 For more look at Look at Surak K. (2013), pp.57-90

16 Look at Chang K. (2015)

17 Look at Japanese Tea Instructors Association (2015), pp.1-72 (in Japanese)

18 Look at Japanese Tea Instructors Association (2015), pp.1-72 (in Japanese)

19 Look at Japanese Tea Instructors Association (2015), pp.1-72 (in Japanese)

20 Look at Japanese Tea Instructors Association (2015), pp.1-72 (in Japanese)

21 Look at Japanese Tea Instructors Association (2015), pp.1-72 (in Japanese)

22 Look at Japanese Tea Instructors Association (2015), pp.1-72 (in Japanese)

23 Look at Japanese Tea Instructors Association (2015), pp.1-72 (in Japanese)

Chapter 8

1 Look at Mair V.H., et al. (2009), pp.85-94

2 Look at Anderson J.L. (1991), pp. 23-32

3 Look at Mair V.H., et al. (2009), pp.85-94

4 Look at Genshitsu S. et al. (2011), pp.85-94

5 Look at Mair V.H., et al. (2009), pp.95-107

6 Look at Genshitsu S. et al. (2011), pp. 24-48

7 Look at Hirota D. (1995), pp.63-79

8 Look at Genshitsu S. et al. (2011), pp. 94-132

9 Look at Mair V.H., et al. (2009), pp. 94-132

10 Look at Anderson J.L. (1991), pp. 49-75

11 Look at Genshitsu S. et al. (2011), pp. 24-48

12 Look at Genshitsu S. et al. (2011), pp. 94-132

13 Look at Surak K. (2013), pp.91-118

14 Look at Surak K. (2013), pp.91-118

15 Look at Genshitsu S. et al. (2011), pp. 94-132

16 Graham P. (2001), pp.137-166

17 Graham P. (2001), pp.137-166

Chapter 9

1 Look at Farris W.W. (1998)

2 Look at Seton A. (2012), pp.205-277

3 Look at Sawada T. (1982)

4 Look at Munsterberg H. (2010), pp.32-55

5 Look at Cort L.A. (2000)

6 Look at Munsterberg H. (2010), pp.32-55

7 Look at Munsterberg H. (2010), pp.32-55

8 Look at Cort L.A. (2007), pp.61-85

9 Look at Kawano R. (1983)

10 Look at Munsterberg H. (2010), pp.32-55

Bibliography

Anderson J.L. (1991). *An introduction to Japanese Tea Ritual*, State University of New York Press: Albany

Banerjee, B. (1992). Botanical Classification of Tea. in K.C.Willson and M.N.Clifford (eds.) (1992). *Tea Cultivation to Consumption*. Yorkshire: Springer Science and Business Media Dordrecht

Battle, V. (2017). Brewing and Drinking tea. *World Tea Encyclopedia: The World of Tea Explored and Explained from Bush to Brew*. Leicestershire: Troubador Publishing

Blair R. (2012). *Organic Production and Food Quality: A Down to Earth Analysis.*, Wiley-Blackwell: Chichester, Oxford

Bryan J. (2008). Psychological Effects of Dietary Components of Tea: Caffeine and L-theanine. *Nutrition Reviews* 66(2), pp.82-90

Chacko S.M., Thambi P.T., Kuttan R. and Nishigaki I. (2010). Beneficial Effects of Green Tea: A Literature Review. *Chinese Medicine* 5(13), pp.1-13

Chang K. (2015). World Tea Production and Trace: Current and Future Development. FAO UN

Chu D.C., Kobayashi K., Juneja L.R. and Yamamoto T., (1997). Theanine – its synthesis, isolation, and physiological activity, in Yamamoto T, Juneja LR, Chu DC and Kim M. (eds.) (1997). *Chemistry and Applications of Green Tea*. Boca Raton: CRC Press

Cort L.A. (2000). *Shigaraki: Potters' Valley*, Weatherhill

Cort L.A. (2007). Shopping for Pots in Momoyama Japan., in Pitelka M. (ed.) *Japanese Tea Culture: Art History and Practice*, Routledge: London and New York, pp.61-85

Deng W.W., Ogita S. and Ashihara H., (2008). Biosynthesis of theanine (γ -ethylamino-l-glutamic acid) in seedlings of Camellia sinensis. *Phytochemistry Letters* 1, pp.115-119

Farris W.W. (1998). *Sacred Texts and Buried Treasures: Issue in the Historical Archeology of Ancient Japan.*, University of Hawaii Press

Friedman M., Lewin C.E., Lee S.U. and Kozukue N. (2008). Stability of Green Tea Catechins in Commercial Tea Leaves during Storage for 6 Months. Journal of Food Science 74(2), pp. H47-H51

Friedman M. (2007) Overview of Antibacterial, Antitoxin, Antiviral and Antifungal activities of Tea Flavonoids and Teas. *Molecular Nutrition and Food Research Journal* 51, pp.116-134

Genshitsu S. and Soshitsu S. (2011). *Urasenke Chado Textbook*, Tankosha

Graham P. (2001). *Tea of the Sages: The Art of Sencha*, University of Hawaii Press: Honolulu

Graham P. (2003). Karamono for Sencha: Transformations in the Taste for Chinese Art., in Pitelka M. (ed.) *Japanese Tea Culture: Art, History and Practice*, Routledge: London and New York, pp.110-136

Hirota D. (1995). *Wind in the Pines: Classical Writings of the Way of Tea as a Buddhist Path*, Asian Humanities

IFOAM (2017). *Definition of Organic Agriculture*. [online] Available at: https://www.ifoam.bio/en/organic-landmarks/definition-organic-agriculture Accessed on 2017.08.05

IFOAM (2014). *Organic Japan and the Global Organic Network*. Available at http://www.ifoam.bio/sites/default/files/organics_in_japan.pdf [online] Accessed on 2017.08.06

Ikeda S., Nakagawa M. and Iwasa K. (1972). Relationship between Infusion of Green Tea and Soluble Component. Tea Research Journal 37, pp.69-78 (in Japanese)

Japanese Tea Instructors Association (2015). *Japanese Tea Instructors' Study I,* Japanese Tea Instructors Association, (in Japanese)

Japanese Tea Instructors Association (2015). *Japanese Tea Instructors' Study III,* Japanese Tea Instructors Association, (in Japanese)

Japanese Tea Instructors Association (2013). J*A Book to Understand Everything about Japanese Tea,* Japanese Tea Instructors Association, (in Japanese)

Jarup L. (2003). Hazards of Heavy Metal Contamination. *British Medical Bulletin* 68(1) pp.167-182

JONA (2017). *JONA Organic Standards 2017.* [online] Available at http://www.jona-japan.org/form/JONA_Standards.pdf Accessed on 2017.08.07

Kawano R. (1983). *Hagi: Famous Ceramics of Japan.*, Kodansha Amer

Kirchmann H., Bertstrom L., Katterer T. Andren O. and Andersson R. (2008). Can Organic Production Feed the World? In Kirchmann H. and Berstrom L. (eds.) *Organic Crop Production – Ambission and Limitations,* Springer, pp.38-73

Kristiansen P., Acram T. and Reganold J. (2006). *Organic Agriculture: A Global Perspective,* CRISCO Publishing: Collingwood, CABI Publishing: Oxon

Lin Y.S., Tsai Y.J., Tsay J.S and Lin J.K (2003). Factors Affecting the levels of Tea Polyphenols and Caffeine in Tea Leaves. *Journal of Agriculture and Food Chemistry,* 51, pp1864-1873

Mair V.H., and Hoh E. (2009). *The True History of Tea,* Thames and Hudson: London

Monhanpuria P., Kumar V. and Yadav S.K. (2010). Tea Caffeine: Metabolism, Functions and Reduction Strategies. *Food Science and Biotechnology* 19(2), pp.275-287

Munsterberg H. (2010). *Ceramic Arts of Japan: A Handbook for Collectors,* Turtle Publishing

Murai Y. (1989). The Development of Chanoyu: Before Rikyu. In Varley P. and Kumakura I. (eds.) Tea in Japan: Essays on the History of Chanoyu, University of Haway Press: Honololu, pp.3-32

OFRF. *Organic FAQs.* [online] Available at: http://ofrf.org/organic-faqs Accessed on 2017.08.06

Okano, K., Chutani, K., Matsuo, K. (1997). Suitable Level of Nitrogen Fertilizer for Tea (Camellia sinensis L.) Plants in Relation to Growth, Photosynthesis, Nitrogen Uptake and Accumulation of Free Amino Acids. *Japanese Journal of Crop Science* 66 (2), pp.279-287

Ostalova M., Tremlova B., Pokorna J. Kral M. (2014) Chlorophyll as an Indicator of Green Tea Quality. *Acta Veterinaria Brno* 83, pp.S103-S109

Othieno, C.O. (1992). *Soils.* in K.C.Willson and M.N.Clifford (eds.) (1992). *Tea Cultivation to Consumption.* Yorkshire: Springer Science and Business Media Dordrecht, pp.137-173

Pani B. (2007). *Textbook of Environmental Chemistry*, I.K International Publishing House: Delhi, Mumbai, Bangalore

Robertson G.L (1998). *Food Packaging: Principles and Practices*, Marcel Dekker: New York, Basel

Sawada T. (1982). *Tokoname, Famous ceramics of Japan, VII*, Kodansha Amer: Tokyo

Sawamura S., Haraguchi Y., Ikeda H., Sonoda J. (2010). Properties and shapes of Matcha With Various Milling Method. *Nippon Shokuhin Kagaku Kogoku Kaishi*. 57(7), pp.304-309 (in Japanese)

Seton A. (2012). *Collecting Japanese Antiques*, Turtle Publishing

Surak K. (2013). *Making Japan: Cultural Nationalism in Practice, Stanford University Press*: Stanford

Tanihata A. (1984). Tea and Kyoto Ceramics in the Late Edo Period. *Chanoyu Quarterly* 37, pp7-27

Varnam A. and Sutherland J.M. (1994). *Beverages: Techonology, Chemistry and Microbiology*, Springer Science and Business Media:

Voung Q.V., Bowyer M.C. and Roach P.D. (2011). L-Theanine: Properties, Synthesis and Isolation from Tea. *Journal of the Science of Food and Agriculture* 91(11), pp.1931-1939

Velayutham P., Babu A. and Liu D. (2008). Green Tea Catechin and Cardiovascular Health: An Update. *Current Medical Chemistry* 15(18), pp.1840-1850

Wolfram S. (2007). Effects of Green Tea and EGCG on Cardiovascular and Metabolic Health. *Journal of the American College of Nutrition* 26(4), pp.373S-388S

Yasunari T.J., Stohl A., Hayano R.S.,Burkhart J.F., Eckhardt S. and Yasunari T. (2011). Cesium-137 Deposition and Contamination of Jpanaese Soils due to the Fukushima Nuclear Accident. Proceedings of the National Academy of Science 108(49), pp 19530-19534

Index

95